ROW BY ROW

ROW *by* ROW

TALKING WITH
KENTUCKY GARDENERS

KATHERINE J. BLACK

Photographs by Deirdre A. Scaggs

SWALLOW PRESS
OHIO UNIVERSITY PRESS

Athens, Ohio

Swallow Press
An imprint of Ohio University Press, Athens, Ohio 45701
ohioswallow.com

Front matter photography:
(page ii) Dorothy Arthur's garden in Scott County
(page vi) Canned produce in Dorothy and Forest Harrison's home, Todd County
(page x) Winged bean, *Psophocarpus tetragonolobus*, grown by Dave Kennedy, Madison County
(page xvi) Seedlings started by Janice Musick, Whitley County
Cover design, author photo, and map by Nyoka Hawkins

To obtain permission to quote, reprint, or otherwise reproduce or distribute material
from Swallow Press / Ohio University Press publications, please contact our rights
and permissions department at (740) 593-1154 or (740) 593-4536 (fax).

"A Mother's Beans: Tom Collins" has previously appeared as "Tom Collins: A Mother's
Beans" in *Appalachian Heritage,* Fall 2012, vol. 40, no. 4, and is reprinted here by
permission of the editor.

25 24 23 22 21 20 19 18 17 16 15   5 4 3 2 1

Library of Congress Cataloging-in-Publication Data
Black, Katherine J., author.
Row by row : talking with Kentucky gardeners / Katherine J. Black.
  pages cm
Includes bibliographical references.
ISBN 978-0-8040-1161-7 (hc : alk. paper) — ISBN 978-0-8040-1162-4 (pb : alk.
paper) — ISBN 978-0-8040-4066-2 (pdf)
1. Gardening—Kentucky. 2. Gardeners—Kentucky—Interviews. I. Title. II. Title:
Talking with Kentucky gardeners.
SB453.2.K4B53 2015
635.09769—dc23

2015022114

For my parents,

Barbara Stier Black (1914–1998) *and*

Charles Rufus Black Jr. (1913–2002),

who taught me how to raise, preserve,

cook, and serve food.

CONTENTS

Acknowledgments
xi

Introduction: *Breaking Ground*
1

Peace of Mind: *Gladys and Walsa Blanton*
13

Back and Forward: *Jashu, Kasan, and Seema Patel*
21

Fidelity: *Dorothy and Forest Harrison*
30

"Can and Dry and Pickle": *Mae Raney Sons*
35

"Da Muchas Vueltas la Vida" (Life, It Takes a Lot of Turns):
Maria and Ciro Prudente
45

Can Do: *Rossneau Ealom*
51

"I Don't Have a Memory That's Not a Garden": *Jennifer Eskew*
58

The Garden of Beautiful Persons: *Marisol Ortiz*
63

The Grace of Soil: *Donna and Larry Haire*
69

Arvilla: *Aaron Mansfield*
77

Divine Land: *Mattie and Bill Mack*
85

A Mother's Beans: *Tom Collins*
93

Live Simply: *Janice Musick*
98

On a Mission: *Joe Trigg*
105

The Lucky Cross: *Gary Millwood*
115

Waste Not, Want Not: *Linda Rose*
123

Leafy Greens Are Where It's At: *Dave Kennedy*
131

Inside Out: *Seema Capoor and Ashish Patel*
143

Of Onions and Time: *Gloria and Don Williams*
149

"The Land Is Good Here": *Martha Barrios and Adan Nuñez*
154

The End of the Road Out Here: *Valeria and Paul Riley*
159

"Raised to Work": *Betty Decker*
169

The Family Who Lives in the Garden: *Saunda Richardson Coleman*
176

The Worth of a View: *Jose Meza*
182

You Can't Buy a Garden, a Good Neighbor, or a Past: *Bev May*
187

The Lesson of *Nhan* and *Hong: Thai Tran*
195

The Tomato Rebellion: *Bill Stewart*
201

Epilogue: *Belonging*
208

Notes
213

Map of Kentucky: The gardeners featured in *Row by Row*
10-11

ACKNOWLEDGMENTS

Little in this world is done on our own. Each gardener in *Row by Row* learned how to grow food from a family member, neighbor, or county extension agent. Some raised their gardens on land that has been handed down through the generations, while others began their gardening lives on a loaned plot. Likewise, what these gardeners grow and how they grow it is not an independent decision but the result of a seed passed along, a tip revealed, a meal shared. Making a book is no different. Many people helped me, and I want to fully acknowledge them.

Janet Eldred read the sabbatical proposal that contained the germ of this project. She helped me organize my thoughts and also encouraged me to think of the oral histories as a larger book project from the beginning. Janet also read early versions of some of the gardeners' portraits and provided me with crucial critique and advice that helped me stay the course.

Dwight Billings, once my professor but also my colleague at the University of Kentucky, provided encouragement and helped me theoretically frame a scholarly paper using some of the first interviews I conducted. The intellectual foundation of that early work guided my thinking as I began to create profiles of the gardeners for *Row by Row*. Jim Minick, a colleague in Appalachian studies, then at Radford University, also gave early support and encouragement. Penny Camp, a dear friend for over forty years, patiently listened to me read early versions of a few pieces and then told me the truth. Her honesty and belief in the project sustained me. Rona Roberts introduced me to Betty Decker, who is profiled in *Row by Row*. Betty was one of the first people I interviewed, and both she and Rona are due heartfelt thanks. Leslie Guttman also stepped in at an early stage, offering skilled and generous editorial assistance. In five minutes, with her journalist's quick eye and sense of a story, she moved early drafts closer to final ones. We hardly knew each other at the time, which makes her generosity all the more remarkable.

Gillian Berchowitz of Ohio University Press took an interest in these garden stories before they had much shape. I appreciate her patience and care and attention as she shepherded the manuscript through the publishing process. She is forthright, with a pithy sense of humor, two qualities that I find admirable and necessary in a working relationship. I am also grateful to Managing Editor Nancy Basmajian and Production Manager Beth Pratt, who turned the manuscript into a book—swiftly, diplomatically, expertly.

Mark Johnson, who doesn't grow a garden but plants connections everywhere he can, contributed immeasurably to *Row by Row*. He introduced me to Louie Rivers Jr. of Kentucky State University's Small Farmer Outreach Program. Without Mr. Rivers's help and confidence in me, this work would be less rich and less true. He connected me with many of the African American gardeners and also put me in contact with Wanda Miick of the Russell County Hispanic Gardening Project. I interviewed three participants in this Kentucky State University and University of Kentucky Cooperative Extension program. Another staff member in the Russell County office, Margie Hernandez, a native of McCreary County, Kentucky, interpreted in Spanish and English during the interviews. Without her language skills, these interviews would never have happened.

Colleague and friend Denise Ho introduced me to Tuan Anh Vu of the Asia Institute–Crane House in Louisville, Kentucky. He helped me meet Thai Tran, the youngest and perhaps most ambitious gardener profiled in this volume. Thai and his wife, Jacinda, have become my friends. I learn from them and I believe in a healthy future for our Earth because of them. Dear friend Doug Burnham introduced me to Tommy Harrison, who was the 4-H agent in Muhlenberg County. He located gardeners in

Western Kentucky for me to interview, including his parents, Dorothy and Forest Harrison.

Librarians and archivists at the University of Kentucky contributed to this project throughout its course. Gwen Curtis of the Maps Department and Roxanna Jones, government documents librarian extraordinaire, both tracked down answers to, at times, arcane questions. They have always been two of my library heroes. The staff of the Louie B. Nunn Center for Oral History lent technical support from the beginning. Director Doug Boyd provided interviewing equipment and used his modest budget to have some of my earliest interviews transcribed. He also located a transcriptionist to translate interviews conducted in Spanish and English. These latter transcriptions were essential to me, a non-Spanish speaker. Sara Abdmishani Price, the Center's Collection Coordinator, was always a bright, competent, and helpful presence. Kopana Terry, who continues Sara's work, has also come to my aid more than once. Three faculty in the University Libraries showed me—over and over—what it means to be a good colleague and friend. I can't thank Carla Cantagallo, Reinette Jones, and Jeff Suchanek enough for their consistent interest, encouragement, and assistance. Each improved the manuscript tenfold by making suggestions, asking questions, and magically changing a word here and a word there to polish my writing.

Other friends also read portions of the manuscript at various points. They gave honest responses, helped solve writing problems, and told me to keep going. They believed in me and the project and that, indeed, kept me going. I will always be grateful to Rusty Barrett, Srimati Basu, Penny Camp, Nikky Finney, Hang Nguyen, Melynda Price, Rosie Moosnick, Dhananjay (Tiku) Ravat, and Janie Welker—all creative people and loyal friends. Srimati Basu and Tiku Ravat also introduced me to their friends Ashish Patel and Seema Capoor, who then introduced me to Jashu and Kasan Patel, the four of whom are featured in *Row by Row*. When I was confused about the names of several Indian fruits and vegetables, Tiku made authoritative identifications and unraveled their multiple spellings.

I sought the advice of poet Nikky Finney and curator Janie Welker as I was deciding in what sequence the profiles should appear in *Row by Row*. Each is in the position of taking individual pieces and organizing them into a whole. A poet determines which poem follows another in a collection and a curator decides the order of art in an exhibit. Both advised me to "listen" to the pieces and create a flow of conversations, not demographic or thematic categories, and since my own voice figures in many of the profiles, they recommended I begin with the piece that signifies my early Kentucky years and end with one that completes the circle. The profiles in between represent the conversations I have had along the way. Poets and art curators always know best.

Nyoka Hawkins, as always, exceeded any obligations that come with longtime friendship. Her editorial hand made every part of this book stronger, from the introduction to the epilogue. If there's any writing that sings, it is because of her. She also designed the book cover and the map locating where the gardeners live. Like her, both are striking but also effectively communicate the spirit of *Row by Row*. No place exists in Nyoka's world for mediocre design.

Albert Zapata and James Price keep things real. I love Albert's wicked sense of humor, his gorgeous bouquets, and the tasty fideo he makes for me with tomatoes and peppers from my garden. I hope our exchange never ends. When my five-year-old friend, James, rings the front doorbell or comes enthusiastically through the back door, I stop what I am doing. Nothing is more important than being present for him. And since he made his first garden last year with the help of his mother, Melynda, he will soon have his own Kentucky garden story to tell.

Without Kathi Kern *Row by Row* would never have materialized. She advised, listened, conversed, encouraged, believed, read, commented, and edited all along the way, even at times, I am sure, when she least felt like it. Kathi has helped me find my voice in untold ways. She is at the heart of this book because she is my heart.

Finally I want to acknowledge all the gardeners who are not profiled in *Row by Row* but who welcomed me into their homes and gardens and told me about their lives: George and Joetta Goodrich, Bruce Mundy, Diane Rose, Toni Eddleman, Roberta Burnes and John Walker, Mary Lucas Powell and John Poundstone, Ryan Koch, Pam Meade, Kutty Narayanan, Pat Dean, John Jones, Dorothy Arthur, Glenda Moorer, Barbara Napier, Jan Smith, Osman Santos, and the late Mary Andrews. Their stories about, knowledge of, and dedication to raising food informed this project from start to finish. I remain grateful for their presence and their vision.

INTRODUCTION

Breaking Ground

MY FIRST GARDEN MEMORY is of being with my father, Charles Rufus. I was five or six years old, and it was a time before our relationship turned (and remained) contentious. "Come here, Katherine," he called. He was standing in front of his workbench in the "furnace room," which housed a massive hot water heater, central air conditioning and heating units, hand tools, screws, nuts and bolts, flashlights, hunting rifles and shotguns, ammunition, baseball bats and gloves, rubber boots, waders and hand warmers for duck hunting, shoe polish, and seeds. Daddy opened an upper cabinet that I could not reach. There next to the shotgun shells was a large, dark green canister whose original purpose was no longer obvious. He brought it down and removed the lid. "This year I am giving you your own bed. Pick what you want to plant." He splayed pretty seed packets across the workbench, which was just at my eye level. "Go ahead. Pick." I think my choices were mostly flowers. I based my decision probably on the color and shape illustrated on each paper envelope containing its respective seed. I remember only four o'clocks and nasturtiums with certainty. And I remember precisely where my plot was, now well over fifty years ago.

I grew up in northeastern Arkansas in Corning, a small town with a population of approximately 2,500 at the time. Our house, built in 1952, the year I was born, sat on a three-acre parcel of low-lying land at the edge of town. My father, trained as an engineer, had drainage ditches dug around three sides of the property where the vegetable garden was situated. We tended a large, elaborate, productive garden. It was both a source of fresh food—everything from boysenberries, asparagus, and melons to corn, tomatoes, squash, and beans—and a springboard for the moral practice of labor. My father plowed, tilled, and saw to the cultivation throughout the growing season. My mother, Barbara, canned and pickled, made jams and jellies, and froze fruit and vegetables for winter use. My six brothers, my sister, and I picked the berries, grapes, beans, corn, and tomatoes, and we girls helped Mother with food preservation. In the spring we ate tender lettuces, green onions, radishes, and asparagus. During the first three weeks of May, we ate strawberries three times a day. In July and August, beans, corn, tomatoes, cucumbers, squash, and melons were staples on our table.

The strawberry patch is what made our garden stand out among all others in Corning. We were known for our strawberries and our enterprise. Once we displayed our hand-painted sign that read "Fresh Strawberries for Sale 857-6794" in the front yard, the season had officially begun. We sold berries to restaurants—some as far as ten miles away—and to households all over town. When we had excess, after orders had been filled, Daddy or Mother telephoned old customers and solicited new ones. We children picked before we left for school, and Mother often continued into the morning before the heat and other chores called her back into the house. My parents kept meticulous business records on a stenographer's pad. Each strawberry season they recorded how many quarts picked, how many sold and to whom, how much money taken in, and the net profit after deducting for fertilizer and straw mulch and wages to the pickers. Corky also had to be paid from the proceeds. He was an employee at our family's sawmill who, after finishing his shift there, came to work in our garden. Corky spread the fertilizer and mulch and blocked the berries after the fruiting season.

Some customers picked up their orders at our house, but we also delivered. Our strawberries were priced to sell. However, we topped off our quarts with a nice mound, never lined the bottom with inferior fruit, and only sold the freshest berries while keeping back the less desirable

ones for preserves at home, and delivery was prompt and free from the back of our family Cadillac. Daddy said these strategies gave our business a good reputation.

My parents were unlikely gardeners. Mother was from Beloit, Wisconsin, and was shocked by the rural nature of her husband's hometown, where they moved in 1939, a year into their marriage. Charles Rufus's family had settled in Corning in the late 1800s. His entrepreneurial grandfather, J. W. Black, had started over in Arkansas after he lost his family's farm and general store in southern Illinois during the bank panic of 1873. Once in Corning he opened an ice company, a mortuary, and later a pool table factory. He finally settled on a sawmill that today is in its fifth generation of family operation. With J.W.'s launch into business, the family left agricultural pursuits behind. But J.W.'s son, my grandfather, Charles Rufus Black Sr., married Bess Jane Graham, who had grown up in the Ozark Mountains on a subsistence farm. She put her vegetable patch adjacent to their substantial white frame house, both facing Second Street, which was lined with Corning's oldest homes and trees. Daddy learned how to grow food from his mother and how to make money from his father. He tried to pass these skills on to each of his eight children. Of all of us, only my sister and I took to the gardening, but we never developed the drive for profits.

After the last of us children left home in the late 1970s, my parents still continued to make a garden. Its size—half an acre—never decreased, and my mother continued to put up food as if she were still feeding a family of ten. After Mother died that stopped, but Daddy, well into his eighties, hired his grandsons and Corky to plant a garden each spring and to pick and deliver the strawberries, activities Daddy directed from a side porch overlooking his "farm." The last year of his life—at eighty-eight years of age—he laid his garden to rest, marking the retirement of one of the last home vegetable gardeners in our community.

Though I grew up in a gardening family and was taught the skills of food preservation, it was not until shortly after I moved to eastern Kentucky in 1973 that I began to raise a garden on my own without parental design and direction. The art and practice of gardening was alive and well, even if in decline, in eastern Kentucky. Gardening and food preservation still bolstered many household economies in addition to providing the foodstuffs for which Appalachian Kentucky cuisine is noted: green beans, potatoes, corn, blackberries, and apples. Growing eggplant was seen as peculiar, whereas saving several kinds of beans—what now would be called "heirloom beans"—was more or less the norm. Men with tractors would plow and harrow their neighbor's garden for next to nothing, and friendly competitions arose among neighbors over who had the earliest Black Seeded Simpson lettuce or whose tomatoes produced first. In this congenial atmosphere, with skilled gardeners around to advise me and the freedom to experiment, I became a gardener in my own right.

At the same time as I was developing my own gardening practices, I was also being influenced by the radical politics of the 1970s—especially feminism, environmentalism, and anti-imperialism. My relationship with my conservative, businessman, gardening father only grew pricklier. In eastern Kentucky, though, I was surrounded by young people in the back-to-the-land movement and involved with those empowered by the emergence of Appalachian identity politics, both of which heralded traditional cultural practices such as gardening and canning. In this heady mix of political and cultural upheaval, I felt free, and even compelled, to take up organic gardening. I came to believe, and still do, that my responsibility is to improve the land while tending it. Growing my food organically was also another realm in which I could rebel against my father, who used chemical fertilizers, insecticides, and fungicides with abandon. And yet, looking back, I think I reasoned that by using organic methods I need not reject gardening, and if I could garden then the one positive tie I had to my father would not be broken.

Since 1986 I have lived in Lexington. I have had two homes, neither of which came with a garden. I had to make them. Each has been smaller than my family's garden and the ones I tended in eastern Kentucky. Because of space considerations, I no longer grow corn, and I use large containers and raised beds to increase the dimensions of my garden. With these amendments I am able to raise a variety of fruits and vegetables: tomatoes, potatoes, greens and lettuces, onions, radishes, asparagus, broccoli, cucumbers, summer and winter squash, herbs, carrots, peas, beans, blackberries, raspberries, and rhubarb. I am attempting to grow blueberries in the Bluegrass region's alkaline soil when they actually thrive in an acidic one. I still can and freeze as my mother taught me. And five years ago I started keeping bees to move toward a more complete backyard ecosystem.

When my brothers and sister and I sold our family home in 2002, the new owners mowed our gardens down. Fifty-year-old asparagus and blueberry bushes. The bramble berries and grapes. Row after row of strawberries. They even cut down the plum and apple trees. The last and only time I saw my homeplace, a huge lawn had replaced all we had built.

I think this destruction has made me a more determined gardener. I want to grow as much food as I can. I continue to grow organically and do not use genetically modified seeds. In a small way, I am saying no to corporate agriculture and food distribution. But gardening, for me, is something more than an expression of anticorporate politics. It is pleasurable—both the physical labor and the sweet taste of fresh food. And the older I get, the more I want to keep my parents close, to bring the best in them into my everyday life. In my mind, one of the most important ways in which we were connected as a family was through growing food, preserving it, and then cooking and eating it together.

How, I wondered, do other vegetable gardeners view their garden work? Are we swimming upstream against corporate agriculture? Is gardening a dying art? Why do people garden when they could buy their food at the grocery store, a food co-op, or a farmers' market? Why do all that heavy, hot work while depending on the vagaries of nature? And why do it, year after year, regardless of the state of the economy? Is gardening a form of resistance to the cultural and economic power of capitalized consumption? Does it reengage or maintain a cultural connection to the past? What forms of satisfaction or pleasure come from working the soil to grow food? Is there a spiritual dimension? What multiple meanings might be found in the act of growing food in our own backyards, creek bottoms, plots, and fields? These are the questions that preoccupied me as I contemplated what we could learn about our history and culture if we listened to gardeners.

Kentucky is a rich place to gather the oral histories of gardeners. Writers such as Harriette Arnow and Wendell Berry have shown us how our communities, our stories, and our land are powerfully and irrevocably connected. We have stayed rural longer than some other places, managing somehow to maintain a few traditional agricultural practices. This lingering agrarian ethos is partly attributable to tobacco, a crop whose cultivation by the late twentieth century varied little (with the exception of the use of chemicals) from practices employed before World War II. Today few small farmers grow tobacco, once Kentucky's signature crop, in part because the federal government no longer subsidizes price supports in the form of poundage quotas and acreage allotments. But through the U.S. Department of Agriculture's Tobacco Transition Payment Program, many former tobacco growers have used the "buyout" money to transition to other crops. Many of these family farmers moved quite successfully into vegetable production and now supply Kentucky's growing number of farmers' markets as well as their own tables. Still others quit farming altogether but maintained the tradition of a home vegetable garden.

Other historical forces have affected Kentucky's landscape. Parts of eastern and central Kentucky attracted a significant number of young people who as part of the back-to-the-land movement in the 1970s were interested—for survival's sake as well as for culture's sake—in learning how to live gently and simply without abusing the earth's resources. Kentuckians have cultivated these, at times, uneasy alliances in which traditional forms are taught to newcomers, who have reinvigorated and even reshaped the practices but, at the same time, kept them alive.

Immigration patterns and the local foods movement have also influenced the current gardening climate in Kentucky. In more recent years, Mexicans, Central Americans, Japanese, Vietnamese, and South Asians have become new Kentuckians. Some have cultivated their own beloved vegetables and introduced their gardening styles, while others, inspired by their new neighbors, have begun to grow food for the first time. The local foods movement has been firmly embraced by many Kentuckians. It is a natural connection because "local" has long been revered in Kentucky. Kentuckians who have raised gardens and preserved food all their lives may not see themselves as part of a movement, but in fact the tenets of "local food" have always guided their lives. Consumers who shop at a community farmers' market are also asserting that local food production, distribution, and consumption are the best sustainable practices for the economy and the environment. Using money from the 1998 tobacco company settlement, Kentucky's Department of Agriculture built on this sensibility. In addition to assisting tobacco farmers' transition to growing other crops, the department also provided valuable marketing by creating the "Kentucky Proud" brand for locally produced foods. These products can be found in farmers' markets, at orchards and roadside stands, and even in supermarkets across the state. Sounding the "local foods" horn helps consumers be more conscious of Kentucky's agricultural present and, I believe, subtly encourages home vegetable gardening and eating.

Kentucky's cultural past and present make it an ideal place to explore how vegetable gardeners have interfaced with continuity and change. How and what we eat is part economy, part culture, part environment, and part biography. How we cultivate a garden and what we raise in it are also mediated by the same contingencies. Gardens, like people, may share a common terrain while wildly diverging from one another in form and content. The Kentucky gardeners profiled in *Row by Row* are an antidote to the tired old stereotypes about what kind of people make Kentucky their home and why. They reflect a diversity of gardening practices, traditions, innovations, and philosophies over the past one hundred years. Their gardens share a Kentucky backdrop, but their life stories have as many colors, shapes, and tastes as heirloom tomatoes do. This book is a meditation on how gardeners make sense of their lives through their gardens. Each profile illustrates how gardening shapes a life and, conversely, how a life shapes the garden.

In the fall of 2008, I began crisscrossing Kentucky interviewing home vegetable gardeners. After two and half years, I had completed over forty recorded oral histories with gardeners from all parts of this region-conscious state. I talked with older and younger people and those in-between. I included those who have spent their lives in Kentucky and others, like myself, who are not native. Also represented in this book are gardeners who are varied in their gardening ways—those who garden in city and small town backyards, who carve out plots from their farmland, and who have sprawling gardens in creek bottoms and former pastures. One of the city gardeners, for instance, grew her vegetables in used five-gallon drywall mud buckets placed near her driveway. The gardeners varied in how they used their produce as well, with a few people both growing for home use and, periodically, selling at their local farmers' market.

I made a second visit to each gardener during the growing season, taking along photographer Deirdre Scaggs, who captured the gardeners in and around their gardens. After these sessions, we were often sent home with whatever was freshest in the garden, canned goods, and treasured seeds. Gardeners are generous.

Friends and acquaintances who do not necessarily share my passion for gardening supported this project with their enthusiasm and valuable help. They generously put me in contact with many of the vegetable gardeners whom I interviewed or with others who could provide an introduction to a gardener. Sometimes when I arranged an interview with one gardener, that person introduced me to another—a neighbor, a fellow seed saver, a colleague in Kentucky State University's Small Farmer Outreach Program.

I also interviewed a few gardeners who were my old friends. A co-worker at the University of Kentucky Libraries, where I worked as the curator of the Appalachian Collection for many years, wanted to be included. And after the *Lexington Herald Leader* published a story about my project, a woman e-mailed and asked me to interview her grandmother.

One winter Sunday I was interviewing Bev May in her Floyd County home after a lunch she had prepared with ingredients from her summer garden. She was a busy nurse practitioner with her own clinic in Hazard, nearly an hour's commute one way. When I asked why she grew a garden, she answered me with a question: "If you have a piece of land, why wouldn't you have a garden?" This is what my father taught me when he gave me a garden plot, a bond between us all our lives even though we rarely saw eye to eye on much else. *Row by Row* is about people whose lives have come from many directions but meet in the garden. Whether they own two hundred acres or no land at all, together they seem to be echoing Bev's sentiment. Indeed, why wouldn't you raise a garden?

KENTUCKY

The gardeners featured in Row by Row *cultivate their home gardens in nineteen of Kentucky's 120 counties.*

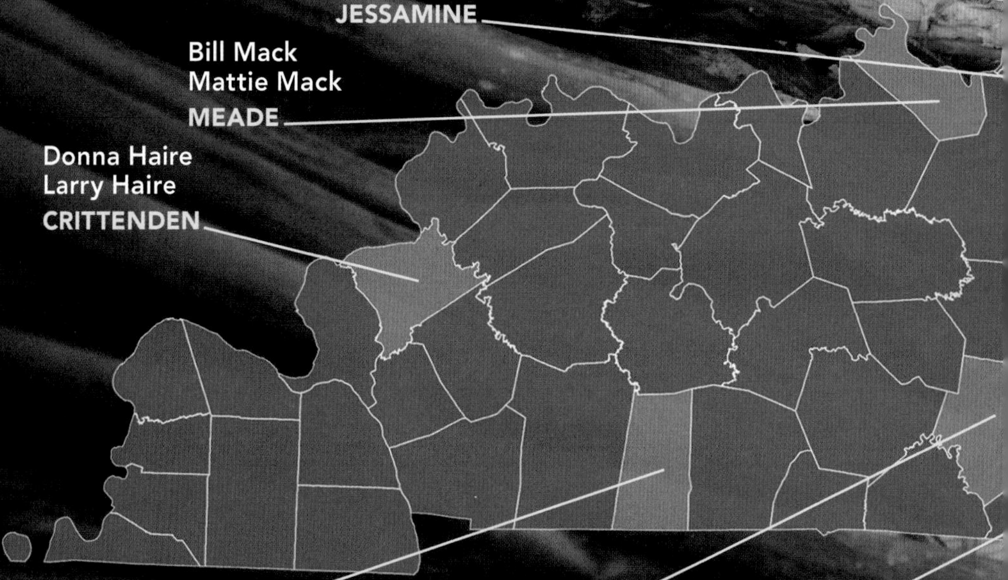

Saunda R. Coleman
Tom Collins
Jennifer Eskew
Aaron Mansfield
Bill Stewart
FAYETTE

Gary Millwood
Thai Tran
JEFFERSON

Jose Meza
JESSAMINE

Bill Mack
Mattie Mack
MEADE

Donna Haire
Larry Haire
CRITTENDEN

TODD
Rossneau Ealom
Dorothy Harrison
Forest Harrison

BARREN
Joe Trigg

RUSSELL
Martha Barrios
Adan Nuñez
Marisol Ortiz
Ciro Prudente
Maria Prudente

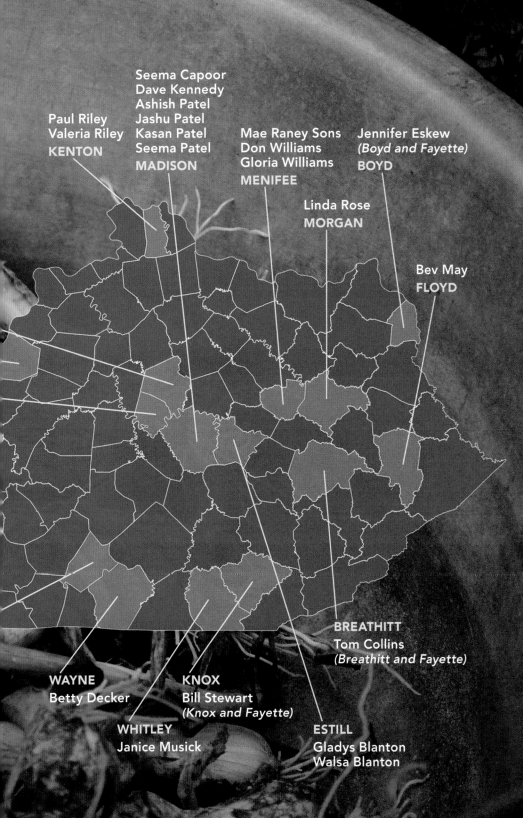

Paul Riley
Valeria Riley
KENTON

Seema Capoor
Dave Kennedy
Ashish Patel
Jashu Patel
Kasan Patel
Seema Patel
MADISON

Mae Raney Sons
Don Williams
Gloria Williams
MENIFEE

Jennifer Eskew
(Boyd and Fayette)
BOYD

Linda Rose
MORGAN

Bev May
FLOYD

BREATHITT
Tom Collins
(Breathitt and Fayette)

WAYNE
Betty Decker

KNOX
Bill Stewart
(Knox and Fayette)

WHITLEY
Janice Musick

ESTILL
Gladys Blanton
Walsa Blanton

PEACE OF MIND

Gladys and Walsa Blanton

I LOVE THE BLANTONS. I have loved them for over thirty years. We met in Estill County, where I moved to direct the public library in the fall of 1978. I rented a house on Crooked Creek, and the Blantons were my neighbors. But it took their teenage sons, who tested my patience one afternoon, to bring us all together as friends.

I started out as something of a curiosity—a single woman living alone in a big old farmhouse eight miles from town, without plumbing and with a coal stove for heating. My first winter there was lonesome. I was twenty-six years old, and all my friends lived either in the coalfields of eastern Kentucky or in Lexington. Estill County was in between and I knew no one. But with spring, new possibilities emerged on Crooked Creek. For one, I noticed a pack of teenagers who often walked up the road, talking, laughing, heading to Arvin's Grocery. One day, while I was out front working up a flower bed, one of the boys in the group whistled at me. I turned swiftly, wagged my finger at him as I walked toward the road, and warned, "Don't you whistle at me. I am a feminist." He burst out laughing, a kind of laugh that admires, not demeans. He was Arnold Blanton, the second-oldest child of Gladys and Walsa. I saw that he was about fifteen years old, and what had seemed like a threat moments before turned into a spunky act by someone alive, curious, and unafraid.

Arnold and his younger brother, Richard, became my first friends in Estill County. They taught me about who was who in the county, where to pick wild blackberries, and who sold the best fresh eggs and milk. Our friendship was cemented when I learned both boys were gardeners. Eventually they took me to a family get-together at their home. Both Gladys and Walsa come from large families, so I walked into a serious gathering, noisy and festive. Besides the table full of desserts, what I most remember about that day is how I felt being around the Blantons and Gladys's people, the Olivers. They were so confident in themselves, in their circle—it was not the confidence that breeds boastfulness but one that might be closer to satisfaction, something that might even result in peace of mind. I recognized it mainly because I did not have it and most likely wanted it. Later, I came to understand that on that day Gladys and Walsa had sized me up and taken me in. For them it was simple: if their children liked me, that was all they needed to know.

As a boy, Walsa (how people say it sounds like "Walsie"), who was born in 1939 in Clark County, moved frequently between farms in Clark, Estill, and Madison Counties. His family were tenant farmers, raising tobacco and corn for the landowners. In exchange, they received a house and garden space where they grew what I have come to call the Kentucky Trinity— potatoes, corn, and beans—along with tomatoes, greens, and onions. Walsa had one older brother, Benny, and nine sisters. "We had it pretty rough. We didn't have a whole lot," he told me quietly, simply. "We never went to town. We didn't have transportation. We walked mostly. We stayed on the farm all the time. When me and Benny got up to ten years old, why, we plowed and everything. We went to farming. Yeah, when I was probably twelve years old, I cut and shocked fodder all night for about fifty cents a shock."[1] He and Benny had to cut wood for the heating and cooking stoves and "pack [carry] water" from the well out back. Tobacco growing brought other chores. "We'd go to the tobacco fields—we were just little fellers— and we'd sucker tobacco all day, maybe, for a couple of dollars a day."[2] The boys would give their parents what they had earned for grocery money after they saved enough to purchase "a pair of shoes and a pair of britches. That'd do us," he said, a forthright assessment of his childhood's material reality.

He spoke with knowledge and pride when he instructed me about how the tobacco beds were sterilized in late winter to prepare for planting the tiny seeds that would become the plants to be set out in fields in May. In Walsa's youth, the custom was to burn the beds; later the preferred method became gassing. Either way the seedbed is sterilized to kill any lingering soil diseases and dormant weeds. "You'd cut wood and stack it up in the beds," Walsa recounted. "And burn it." Sometimes a large piece of woven wire fencing would first be laid on the bed, and then "they'd pile the wood on there and set it on fire. Then they'd hook the mule to it and move it up till they got the whole bed burnt." In late February or early March, this necessary ritual was practiced all over Kentucky, wherever burley tobacco was grown. After a long winter, burning the beds was also a chance to socialize. "We'd sit around. And [people would] tell big tales and would carry on, joke and everything while the fire was burning." Once the tobacco seeds were planted in the sterilized beds, lettuce seeds and tomato seeds were placed on the edges, and then all was covered with a canvas, allowing the soil to warm up to activate germination. As I learned from so many gardeners who also grew up raising tobacco, the garden and the tobacco crop often went hand in hand.

At seventeen years old, Walsa left home, lived with a neighbor, and began seeking farmwork. Even though I have known him many years, I had never before heard Walsa talk so openly about his childhood. Summing up his conditions, Walsa told me, "You didn't make nothing much. You lived, barely, and that's about it." As Walsa embarked on an adult life, one that might not have looked all that different from his childhood, he met Gladys at a neighbor's house. If the saying "opposites attract" is true, then Gladys and Walsa are proof. While Walsa is reticent, Gladys is an unabashed talker whose ready laughter punctuates her sentences and creates transitions of feeling. Walsa and I had started the interview without her because she was in town doing errands. She returned home to join us at the very point in Walsa's story that she had actually entered his life. It was a dramatic entrance, signature Gladys.

Gladys's family also farmed other people's land, never owning any of their own. But Gladys pointed out that not all tenant farmers are the same. "We were a lot richer than Walsa's family," she offered freely while laughing. That laugh was a polite way of signaling to me that she was about to tell me something I probably had not considered. "Daddy always owned two cows. He had his own cows. His own meat hogs. And always kept a horse. Or a team of mules. But Walsa's daddy never did have a cow or anything like that of his own. I never did in my life as a child know what it was to not sit down at the table with food. We always had milk and butter and eggs. But when Walsa was a child growing up, he said there was times that they wouldn't even have food on the table." In 1959, with those significant distinctions in their backgrounds but with much in common, Gladys, sixteen years old, and Walsa, nineteen, began their marriage. Gladys knew how to grow tobacco—she had hand-set plants with her father. He had also taught her how to raise vegetables: green beans, corn, tomatoes, cucumbers, Irish potatoes, sweet potatoes, beets, peppers (both hot and sweet), and cabbage. As the oldest daughter, she had often helped her mother weed the garden. And she knew how to preserve food. "We always canned apples, made applesauce and apple butter, dried apples." She told me that as a young married couple, "[We] fell into the same pattern like we were raised up. We never did get very far out from under Mommy and Daddy's thumbs because I started having kids and Mommy was still having kids, too. We stayed close to Mommy and Daddy all our lives." Doris, Arnold, Richard, and Lena were born. And in 1979 when I met the Blantons, they were living in a big old white farmhouse on Crooked Creek—the Winkler place—raising tobacco for the owner.

By the time they entered high school, Arnold and Richard were passionate gardeners. They planted the Kentucky Trinity but were also interested in growing cauliflower, broccoli, herbs, and a variety of flowers. When I asked Gladys and Walsa how they taught their children to garden,

Walsa said, "When [we'd] go out there and plant, they'd go along and you let them help plant." Gladys added, "They just followed along. We didn't really see it as being a job, or hard to do. It was just something that fell into place," she concluded, laughing one of her "it was just life" kind of laughs. The truth is, though, that Gladys and Walsa did not want their children's lives to be as hard as theirs were. Richard and Arnold were never allowed to drive the tractor, and while they may have helped with the tobacco crop, they were not suckering the plants all day long in the heat as Walsa had done when he was a boy. Like her mother before her, Gladys taught her children, boys included, how to put up food. But in that household, Arnold's and Richard's interests in flowers and experiments in horticulture were equally as important. They entered flower arrangements and their more unusual vegetables in the county fair contests, winning praise, ribbons, and prize money. Once they asked me if they could have an eggplant from my garden, implying that they were going to prepare it for a meal. Instead they entered it, under their names, in the vegetable category at the fair. I never knew, until years later, that they won a blue ribbon on my eggplant that year. I am fairly sure, though, that it was the only entry in the eggplant category from the entire county and that Arnold and Richard had banked on that.

This sense of creativity and play, and even leisure, that Walsa and Gladys gave their children and that was so utterly different from their own raising was in part possible because Gladys left the farm and got a "public works" job at the nursing home in the county seat of Irvine. With one waged worker in the household, the burden of worrying how well the tobacco would do in a given year or how much money it would bring in was lightened. In 1984 Gladys reshaped their work lives even more dramatically. "I told Walsa, 'You've done this long enough. You're getting you a job.' And he just didn't think that he wanted to give up farming. I took him to the Central Office [of the Estill County Public Schools], helped him fill out an application, and I told them over there, I said, 'He needs a job. He's farmed all his life and I'm tired of it.'" Laughing at her own audacity, she finished, "But anyway, then, they hired him. I tell him all the time that I took him and got him a job." For twenty-three years after, Walsa worked as a custodian at various Estill County elementary schools, beloved by scores of children and teachers. His departure from raising tobacco, though earlier than that of some other Kentucky farmers, was part of a larger exodus. In Estill County alone, the number of acres of tobacco cultivated fell from 1,107 in 1992 to 898 in 1997 to 382 in 2002.[3] Ironically, leaving farming and obtaining waged work allowed the Blantons to buy land for the first time.

In their new home, which sits on three acres, the Blantons had enough room to continue gardening, plant a small orchard, and keep chickens. For a while, a milk cow named Clementine grazed on a hillside by day and relaxed in the old barn by night. I helped Richard plant the pear trees that started the orchard. I watched his moss garden increase in size each year as he painstakingly transported moss from deeper woods to plant in his shade garden. And each time I visited—by then I lived in Lexington— there was a new flower bed, an experimental crop, an exotic fowl, or a beehive.

And always delicious gossip that was dished out with the Sunday dinner. But owning land and making a permanent home never ensures security and well-being, even though deep in the American psyche we equate the two. If only it were true. In all too quick of a succession, Gladys and Walsa lost three of their four children, in the same order that they were born: first Doris, the oldest, in a car accident, then Arnold from an illness, and Richard from a car accident. Doris's son Josh, their first grandchild, was also killed in the accident with his mother.

If owning land cannot stop the nearly unbearable, perhaps using it gently for our sustenance is one way of coping when our lives have been shattered. Gladys spoke tenderly yet frankly about this very subject. "To me, every time I go out back I can see my kids. Doris and Josh. See, we had bought the house a year before they got killed. They have roots here, too. That's where Arnold and Richard, they had their garden. And Richard would say, 'Mommy, this is where I talk to God at, over here in my garden.' And Arnold, he would too. He'd say, 'Mommy, this is where I'm at peace, is whenever I'm gardening.'"

Walsa concurred. "It's peace of mind. You forget about everything else when you are in the garden. Yeah, it's peaceful. You're thankful, thankful that you can do it. As long as I can walk and go, why, I'll always garden."

I have a photograph on my desk that I look at every day. Richard is showing his niece, Kayla, daughter of Lena, the youngest and only living child of the Blantons, how to husk corn. The table is full of beautiful produce from the late summer garden—tomatoes, red and green peppers, and corn, of course. Doris and Arnold had already died when this photograph was made. But Richard is teaching Kayla what she needs to know. I think he was demonstrating what might happen when you grow your own corn, pick it, prepare it, and eat it, year after year, even when you have sustained unspeakable losses. I think he was conveying to Kayla that through this cycle of life forces comes a peace of mind that carries us through. Or as Walsa put it, "I'm still going."

BACK AND FORWARD

Jashu, Kasan, and Seema Patel

BEFORE THEY MARRIED, Jashu and Kasan had known each other all their lives. They had grown up within a mile and a half of each other and attended the same school, and Jashu's brother and Kasan's sister were married to each other. Raised near the village of Bodwank, in the Indian state of Gujarat, Jashu and Kasan share an agricultural past and, like many other Kentuckians, the community and familial ties that are common to rural upbringings.[4] "My parents were small farmers who owned their land," said Jashu. Her family grew sugarcane, rice, and mangoes to sell and vegetables for their own use. But her father was also a teacher, and at harvest time they could afford to hire seasonal laborers. Jashu's earliest memory of working on her family farm was that of picking peanuts. She remembered the job as "easy" and fondly recalled learning how to grow food from her grandparents and parents. Kasan, in contrast, was expected to perform farm chores before and after school and described his family as "poor." They, too, grew sugarcane, rice, and mangoes for the market but kept most of the vegetables for their own subsistence.

By the time of their wedding in 1977, Jashu had turned twenty-one and Kasan was twenty-seven. They were married in Bodwank, but within two years the Patels had arrived in Chicago. There, they lived in an apartment, worked on the assembly line in various factories, and started a family that eventually grew to one daughter and two sons. "Jashu's brother

Papadi bean or hyacinth bean.

applied for us," Kasan explained. He and Kasan's sister were already settled in Chicago and were prepared to sponsor the newly married couple.
Surrounded by concrete and having no earth in which to plant, Jashu
settled for some indoor flowers and houseplants. "I missed it," she said.
Kasan added that to obtain fresh vegetables, they went to "pick-your-own
farms and harvested—outside of the city—bell peppers, beans, tomatoes." Jashu completed the thought: "Just for fun." They were accustomed
to growing much of the food for their table, a cornerstone of their
Bodwank life. Now, in Chicago, they had to make do.

Chicago and other midwestern industrial cities, such as Cleveland,
Cincinnati, Dayton, and Detroit, were common destinations for Kentucky
migrants who left in great numbers during World War II to work in plants
that supported the military effort. The stream of out-migration—people
looking for jobs—continued into the 1960s as the coal mines of eastern
Kentucky mechanized and unemployment rose. And in Kentucky, as elsewhere, the family farm as a sustainable household economy grew more
untenable. When Kentucky out-migrants left their home communities,
they usually headed for a city and a neighborhood where relatives and
other community members had previously established themselves and
could help them find jobs and housing and provide some semblance of
"home." Sociologists and historians call this "chain migration."

Immigrants to the United States, such as Jashu and Kasan, have often
followed these same patterns. But, of course, their journey is more difficult because they must have sponsorship from a financially stable family
member and meet a complicated set of requirements, including country
quotas that expand and contract over time according to political machi-
nations, domestic unemployment, and government and industry needs.
Jashu and Kasan's eligibility to immigrate was determined by radical
policy changes formulated during the Kennedy and Johnson administra-
tions, a time of sweeping, liberal social reform in the United States.

In 1965, Congress passed the Immigration and Nationality Act. Ap-
proved a year after the Civil Rights Act, which outlawed inequalities at

home, the new immigration policy challenged racist quotas that had favored Western European migrants over those from other countries. It also allowed for immigrants to reunite their families by petitioning for a relative to enter and stay in the United States. Finally, the act aimed to attract immigrants with certain kinds of skills. Because the Cold War, Sputnik, and the race to the moon had increased American self-consciousness and fear of lagging behind in science and technology, the government wanted to import more engineers and research scientists. The United States also needed an influx of doctors after the 1965 legislation approving Medicare and Medicaid had significantly increased the number of Americans who could afford medical care.

The preponderance of Indians immigrating to the United States between 1965 and 1977 were doctors, Ph.D. scientists, and engineers. As a mechanical engineer, Jashu's brother, who would later sponsor Jashu and Kasan's immigration, was part of this cohort when he arrived in the United States in 1971. But in 1976 the stream of professionals from India slowed because Congress amended the Immigration and Nationality Act to require migrants to have specific job offers in order to enter the United States. Jashu and Kasan, however, arriving in 1979, met the requirements of the family reunification provision. Jashu and Kasan as well as their family members who followed might be considered the immigration vanguard because "since the 1980s the percentage of technical workers among South Asian migrants has steadily decreased and the percentage of family members who come to make their lives in the United States has grown."[5] Today, Jashu has two brothers and Kasan has four brothers and one sister living in the United States.

After ten years of urban living in Chicago, Jashu and Kasan were finally able to grow their own garden when they moved to Kentucky in 1990. Once again they followed their siblings (who are married to each other), who left Chicago to become motel keepers in Middlesboro, the largest town in southeastern Kentucky. Jashu and Kasan went to Richmond, the home of Eastern Kentucky University, to run a BP gas station.

But by the late 1990s, Jashu and Kasan had left the gas station business, obtained factory jobs, and moved across town, where they bought the house they live in today. Jashu began working for Kukuku Rubber and Kasan for a company that makes car parts. At both houses where they have lived in Richmond, they made backyard gardens to grow tomatoes, okra, eggplant, beans, chili peppers, and other vegetables, such as *karela,* or bitter gourd, common to their Gujarati cuisine. Kasan explained, "You can buy [some of the vegetables we use,] but it is expensive. We do grow beans that you can't buy in Richmond or anywhere [nearby]. If you go to an Indian store, you will find them, but they will be ordered from somewhere and won't be fresh."[6]

The Patels also garden "because," as Jashu said, "it is fun [and] I have a whole year I don't have to buy my green vegetables because I freeze and use [as needed]." I interviewed the Patels in late April, and Jashu pointed out, "Still I have my vegetables in the freezer." In their native India, freezing or other methods of food preservation were not necessary. The households of Jashu and Kasan grew food year round in the mild Gujarati climate and as Kasan pointed out, "Cooking is fresh every day." But in Kentucky, where freezing winter temperatures make year-round growing impossible, putting up food for the cold seasons is a boon, and Jashu is rightly proud of her stores.

Growing food does save the Patels money and provides the vegetables that are essential to their vegetarian diet and cannot easily be found in Richmond. Though their daughter, Seema, who sat in on our interview, agreed, she mused about their gardening more philosophically. It is also "a release for them from a monotonous pace of everyday life," she said. "You can see the fruits of your labor." Kasan, with his low-key demeanor, explained how his day is transformed during gardening season when he comes home from his job each afternoon. "I take a rest for half an hour to forty-five minutes and then do something outside. Sometimes I park my car and I don't come inside first. I just walk around first [looking at my garden]." And even though both Kasan and Jashu

Karela (bitter gourd).

work at physically demanding jobs, when the beans are being harvested, Seema said her parents are out working in the garden "from three o'clock until sundown."

Seema observed, too, that when her mother is cooking dinner she often says, "Oh, this is so fresh. It is from the garden." Seema said, "If [food] is from your garden, you feel a connection to it." That relationship can also have a spiritual quality, and for Jashu, her deep bond with the soil stretches beyond that of growing food. Sometimes in the morning when Seema wakes she sees her mother praying to the family's *tulsi* plant, "a very sacred plant in Hinduism," she told me. Sometimes called Indian basil or holy basil, *tulsi* is an aromatic plant with "healing properties," and it is often a central presence in Hindu households.

While gardening expresses a spiritual connection and practice for many, it can also manifest specific forms of social interaction that are both satisfying and edifying to a gardener. This dynamic is not lost on the Patels. Someone in Jashu's "Indian group," as she calls it, advised her to periodically water her curry leaf plant (*Murraya koenigii*) with diluted Assam black tea, a tip that she believes is the source of her plant's health. One of Jashu's coworkers, a native Kentuckian who farms and raises cattle, provides manure for the Patel garden. And Jashu, especially, enjoys the friendly competition among gardeners, including with her nearby brother-in-law, based on whose vegetables produced the earliest and whose garden is the most productive. Likewise, the shared generosity that often results in exchanging seeds or plants, sometimes with a near stranger, is how gardeners establish rapport. As Seema put it, "You can count on two gardeners to connect, regardless of whatever walks of life they come from."

If Seema is right, and I believe she is, I wonder about expanding the concept of connection. If you come to Kentucky from some other place, and you begin to grow a garden here, does the experience root you more deeply in Kentucky? Do you feel like a Kentuckian, at least in part, be-cause of your connection to the land? I asked this question of several of the immigrant gardeners I interviewed, with varying answers. When I met Seema she was twenty years old and had spent most of her life in Madison County, until she became a student at the University of Louisville. She is the daughter of immigrants—two dedicated Kentucky gardeners—but not a gardener herself. Still, I queried her, "Do you feel like a Kentuckian?" She answered, "What is a Kentuckian, really? I call Kentucky my home, but I'm not connected to the land as much as other people are." Later, she reneged a bit. Even though she sees herself living in Chicago eventually, not Kentucky, she said, "I do want to have my own garden someday. I think gardening is something you have to learn on your own. I mean, you can be taught to do whatever you need to do, but everyone has their own quirks and their own ways of doing things. I think I need to find my own niche."

Could Seema's idea of a niche be parallel to her notion of connection? Is finding your niche akin to finding a piece of what connects you to a spiritually and socially meaningful life? When I had asked Kasan if making a garden here led him to feeling more connected to Kentucky, he said, "We grow a garden to use the vegetables for our own. Plus we have a time for fun and save some money." Seema, however, interjected, "It connects back to the motherland. They both come from extremely agricultural families. They are both connecting back."

Seema is right. Many home vegetable gardeners are re-creating their past—with modifications—to carry on what was passed to them by their families and communities. But I think her parents are also making a path toward the future through their gardening. It is not an exercise of nostalgia to produce the food that is essential for your vegetarian cuisine, to use your mind and body in healthy ways that much of contemporary U.S. society has disavowed, and to show your children a way of being that was foundational for yourself—one that requires hard work, discipline, and knowledge, all the while saving money for their college educations. As both Jashu and Kasan emphasized, growing food is certainly an economic strategy for them just as it was for their parents and grandparents.

Jashu saves seeds, and this act is perhaps the one that is most representative of the connection between her past, present, and future. She saves the ones that are most important to her or that would be the hardest to find in the United States: bitter gourd (or *karela*), okra, and various beans. She showed me her bag of precious seeds. They were all mixed together, but she assured me, "I know which ones are which." I told her that in Kentucky many gardening families save bean seeds, in particular, that there are dozens of local bean strains with colorful names, and that a family's bean might be considered something like sacred to them. Seema said, "I guess that's what makes [my parents] Kentuckians. They do have a particular bean that they grow." Jashu responded by pulling a bean seed from her bag and holding it in her hand. *"Papadi,"* she said, giving its name in Gujarati (it is also sometimes spelled "papdi"). Papadi is a hyacinth bean that grows on a vigorous vine. The Patels plant it at the back of their house, letting it grow more than twelve feet from the ground to an upper balcony along an elaborate trellis made of twine and wood. By midsummer a wall of flowering vines and bean pods hides the walkout basement. And by late summer Kasan must use a ladder to pick beans.

I do not know how many papadi beans you would have to save and how many you would have to grow to help your children attend college or to keep your past alive. But I can imagine how one bean after another, like putting one foot in front of another, can matter. Immigrants and migrants who follow their families and community members in a chain migration are seeking economic opportunity but also cultural sustenance. The Patels' papadi is emblematic of both. Jashu and Kasan have covered many miles—from a rural, agricultural life in Gujarat to their current small-town gardening life in Kentucky. Papadi has made this trek with them. And I feel sure that it will also be with Seema as she looks for connection and for her "niche."

FIDELITY

Dorothy and Forest Harrison

DOROTHY AND FOREST HARRISON have stayed put all their lives.[7] They were born in northern Todd County—Dorothy, in 1928, across the creek and road from where they now live and Forest, in 1923, down the road about two miles in Collier Springs. Dorothy moved once. She was a teenager when her parents bought the farm and moved the family across the road. Forest left once. He was eighteen years old when he went into the army during World War II. After being stationed in the Philippines, Forest returned home to marry Dorothy.

The Harrisons set up housekeeping and in due time began farming the land that belonged to Dorothy's parents and is now theirs. They raised corn, cattle, burley tobacco, and a garden while working other full-time jobs. Forest was employed by the Kentucky Highway Department and Dorothy at the public high school as a secretary. They had two children. Daughter Susan lives on the adjacent farm with her husband. The Harrisons' son, Tommy, is county extension agent for 4-H youth development in Muhlenberg County, the county adjoining Todd, to the north. He calls Forest and Dorothy every day.

Dorothy and Forest have fidelity: to their homeplace, their community, their children, their land, their church, their marriage, and their garden. For them gardening is not really something to be examined, analyzed, or wondered about. A garden has always been part of their

lives. Year after year they have grown one, and with only a few modifications, they have raised the same vegetables year after year. They grow the things they like to eat—tomatoes, beans, corn, squash, a little broccoli and cabbage. Except for using a rototiller and more recently developed pesticides, they cultivate their garden the way they always have, the way their parents did. And even though they no longer raise tobacco, Forest burns off a little strip of earth in early spring to sterilize it; instead of planting a mixture of tobacco and tomato seeds in this traditionally prepared bed, he sows it with only tomato seed.[8] Then he lays a cover of "tobacco cloth" over the bed to maintain warmth for germination and growth. Forest has always started their tomato plants this way.

When I arrived at the Harrisons' home to interview them on a clear, warm day in May, Dorothy greeted me, appearing ten to fifteen years younger than she is, with her schoolgirl figure and quick movements. Forest, who, I was told, had claimed he would not grow any vegetables that year, was out in their massive garden wrestling with a rototiller. It looked almost as large as Forest, but I sensed that ultimately he would prevail. Dorothy announced, looking fresh, that they had been planting before I arrived, because the rain had finally let up. Later, I asked Forest why he keeps gardening, especially since he had recently endured serious health issues. He said, "I really don't know." Dorothy interjected, as she often does, "He hates to admit it, but I know he enjoys it. He likes to show off that pretty, clean garden." She continued, "Most of the time you can't find a weed in it." With barely a pause, Forest said, "I think you will this time." Laughing, Dorothy was delighted with their gentle banter. But while considering the next year's planting season, questioning whether he would put in a garden, Forest mused, "I'm going to try not to but I'm gonna have to."

After a tasty lunch of Dorothy's made-from-scratch cooking and homemade pickles, it was time for me to go. But before I did, Dorothy showed me her pie safe, still lined with last season's canned tomatoes, beans, pickles, and relish. She selected a few jars to send me home with.

Forest and Dorothy both walked me out because, I suspect, that is what they always do with their company. Besides, Forest was set on showing me something, insisting that I walk beyond the carport. He guided me to the exact spot from which a steeple could be observed. It looked as if it were rising out of the distant ridge. Forest said simply, directly, "That's our church." It was Wednesday, and they were going to the evening service.

Attending church twice a week, putting in a garden every year, talking to your grown son every day, seeing your daughter drive down the road for her daily commute, sharing excess garden produce with neighbors, raising your own tomato plants—these all require faith but also express it. The Harrisons are guided by a lifetime of habits—habits they choose, which bring pleasure and meaning to their lives. They are the habits of belonging to a place. Everything they need is right there around them.

"CAN AND DRY AND PICKLE"

Mae Raney Sons

IF I SUDDENLY had to live off the grid or if the world as I know it was coming to an end or if I entered a time machine that took me back to the 1920s, I would want to be with Mae Raney Sons. Born in 1915 to S. B. and Hannah Lee Raney, who owned several farms in Menifee County during the course of her girlhood, Mae remembers how to live well in the old-time way. She knows how to preserve and store food without refrigeration and how to maximize the length of the garden season by using nature's resources. And although over the years she gained electricity, a freezer, and a rototiller, and what was once a means of survival is now a habit of being, she never lost her zeal for the hot, sweaty work of growing a garden and putting up food for the winter. Mae said, "I think it is healthy for the body to get out there and work and sweat. It makes you stronger. That's why I am here at my age, exactly. And [because of] the good Lord, too. You can get out there and work, and you're not only fixing something for yourself or for the neighbor but it's healthy. It's why I do it."

Mae fell in the middle of nine children. Her father was a schoolteacher in local one-room schools. He began teaching in 1900, and as was customary at that time, he passed the state teacher's examination that allowed one to teach with a high school diploma. In Mae's own words, "My dad didn't know anything about farming. My mother was the farmer." In the early part of the twentieth century, eastern Kentucky farms, still oriented toward subsistence, could be quite diverse in crops and live-stock. Mae's memories illustrated how her mother's farming practices fell squarely within this agricultural history.

"I can remember when we had wheat fields," she said, and recalled 'shocking it out.'" Her mother spread out a white sheet on which she beat the stalks to release the husk-enshrined kernels. One of Mae's jobs was to be a "walker." After putting on clean shoes, she and other children walked on the kernels to break the husks so they could be swept away. Mae's mother would "fan the husks away, then stir, and fan again, stir it, and fan again until you had the wheat kernels there. They would take that to the mill and have it ground. Then you could sieve it." According to Mae, the family grew enough wheat to provide most of their own flour needs.[9]

When Mae remembers the wheat growing and her role in producing the household's flour, she pictures, too, the split rail fence that enclosed the field to keep out livestock—theirs and the neighbors'. Mae's family did not have just one milk cow; they had a herd. Besides moving them beyond their own subsistence, having such plenty allowed them to help neighbors in need. Mae remembered, "My dad took this cow to the neighbors'. They had a baby and no milk. I can remember him putting a halter on one of the cows and driving her over and turning [her] over to the neighbors so they could feed their children."

Hogs were also a staple of the household's agricultural economy. While the family raised yellow corn to feed livestock, especially in the winter, hogs on the Raney farm ran free on acres of fenced woods, living off mast.[10] "Back then, there were beech nuts from big beech trees. They are scarce now," Mae said. "There's a blight that's stopped them from [bearing] nuts. Well, the hogs would go and root the leaves back [on the forest floor] and gather them nuts and they would eat them nuts."[11] And when a sow had babies, Mae explained, she made her way out of the woods with the piglets to be fed corn, greatly improving her ability to nurse adequately. The health of the piglets and the sow meant not only that the Raneys would have plenty of pork for their large family but also that the excess could be sold, traded, or shared.

Even people who today do not raise vegetable gardens might be able to imagine how a family of eleven could eat well during the summer months. But at summer's end with fall frosts and freezing winter months looming ahead, the imagination undoubtedly falters. Mae Sons, however, remembers exactly how they did it. "We grew so much stuff, but you didn't have freezers back then. You'd can and dry and pickle," she said. And bury. "We'd hole up our potatoes," she explained. First they would select a well-drained spot and dig a deep hole there. Then they would line the hole with hay, place the potatoes in the sunken bed, and cover them with another layer of hay or straw topped by dirt. The final step was to create a roof over the covered pit by making a fodder shock of cornstalks.[12] Its conical shape shed water away from the storage bin. "And then in the wintertime, if the ground's not frozen," Mae said, "you go out and kindly move the fodder around, and you can open up, go in there, and get you some potatoes, and then you put it all back like it was." And if you were lucky, the potatoes would not rot over the winter, and you would have enough left by springtime to become the "seed potatoes" for the next year's crop. Other root vegetables, such as turnips and rutabagas, were holed up successfully, too, on the Raney farms, though rutabagas were more likely used for cattle feed than for human consumption. Sweet potatoes, which are sensitive to moisture, were individually wrapped in paper, placed in wooden barrels,[13] and kept in the house to avoid freezing. But it was the unusual way, at least to me, that they kept cabbage fresh into the dead of winter that captured my fullest attention.

Cabbage tends to be a late spring or early summer crop in Kentucky. But Mae emphasized that her family strategized to extend the growing season, both in the early spring and into the fall. Having a "late cabbage" crop was part of this strategy. "Before time for it to freeze [and after the cabbage had] headed up, ready to eat," Mae explained, "we'd take the turning plow and turn a row [make a furrow] and pull that cabbage up and put [its] head down into the furrow. Where its roots was, they'd take another furrow and that covered it. All of a sudden the cabbage head became the roots. If it was real cold and they froze, the dirt took the moisture out of the cabbage and [then the cabbage couldn't rot]. If we wanted cabbage when the ground was thawed, we'd just go get it so we could have cooked cabbage [or] coleslaw [or] whatever we wanted." Imagine experiencing the luxury of having a fresh vegetable in January that is not pickled or canned. I wonder if this is why Mae remembered this technique in such detail and wanted to teach me about it.

Fruit was also integral to the family's diet. To start an orchard, first corn was cultivated on a hillside to rid the area of weeds and other sprouts. The following year fruit trees—apples, plums, peaches, pears, and apricots—replaced the cornfield. Mae once observed her mother looking at a photograph of an orchard in a Stark's catalog and heard her say to her father, "We'd never grow anything that looked like that."[14] But later, after she developed their orchard, she said, "It was just like the picture." And productive, too. Mae said that they gave away a lot of fruit because they had "extra" even after canning and drying.

Before sharing apples with their neighbors, though, the Raneys made "bleached apples," so called because the slices stayed white instead of turning brown as a peeled apple does when it is exposed to air. "Bleached apples" were preserved using sulfur before they were dried, and it was the sulfur that prevented browning.[15] Using wooden barrels like the ones for pickling, "you put [the apples] down in a layer in the barrel—a dishpan full of peeled and quartered apples," Mae explained. "You push them [from the center] and line them up against the edge of the barrel. You take an old mug, like you drink coffee out of, and put [some] sulfur in it and then set it afire." To start the fire, the Raneys attached a bolt to a wire, heated the bolt up in a fire, then lowered it into the barrel to ignite the sulfur. The barrel had to be covered quickly "because if you breathed it, sulfur would kill you." They let the sulfur smoke for about three days and then added another layer of apples and

another mug of sulfur, repeating this process as many times as the barrel would still accommodate apples.[16]

Preserving some of summer's abundance by drying apples and extending the growing season in the fall by planting a late crop of cabbage, as the Raneys did, was matched by starting food production as early as possible in the spring. Like many other mountain families in the first half of the twentieth century, they sowed early crops of lettuce, started their own sweet potato slips, and even planted early beans in hopes that the crop could be protected from spring frosts. A pit method was used for the lettuce and sweet potato slips or plants. For the lettuce, Mae described how they dug a sunken bed the size of a discarded window sash at hand, put well-rotted chicken manure in the hole, scattered the seed, and placed the window to span and rest on all sides of the perimeter of the pit, allowing light in while holding in warmth. It was a low-tech greenhouse. She said, "when other people would be a-sowing it, we'd be a-eating it." Preparing a sweet potato bed for starting slips was similar, with a few twists since sweet potatoes are sensitive to cold and frost.[17] Instead of adding well-rotted chicken manure, the sweet potato bed needed the heat that fresh manure creates. But because manure can also burn tender plants, it was covered with a good layer of rich soil (Mae said, "from a hillside where a log has rotted"), after which the slips are placed and covered by another layer of well-rotted dirt. Like the lettuce bed, the sweet potato "pit" is also covered with an old glass window. Planting early "bunch" beans, green beans that grow on bushy plants and do not climb, required less up-front work, but if frost was imminent, the plants had to be covered with burlap bags draped over tobacco sticks. Because green beans may be the single most cherished vegetable for Kentuckians, the Raneys' gamble to produce an early harvest of beans was logical.

Over the course of Mae's girlhood, her parents acquired several farms, one as large as five hundred acres. While S. B. taught at a nearby country school, the family lived on one of their farms until Hannah Raney got it "up and running." Then that farm was turned over to tenants so that the Raney family could begin improvement on another one. This intent and economic advantage set Mae's family apart from many others in her world. She relayed many stories (told as a "matter of fact," not to boast) of her family sharing what they had with others who had less— seeds, fruit, a milk cow, plentiful beans and corn in the fall. "I am not saying we was well off," Mae explained, "but there was a lot of poor people living around us. But we was never taught to look down on any-body. Unh-uh. [My parents,] they'd have skinned us alive."

Mae has carried this egalitarian impulse with her into her nineties. And it still manifests itself in sharing the fruits of her garden. When she reminisced about the "new" vegetables that she has grown in recent de-cades—broccoli, cauliflower, and Brussels sprouts—a story was sparked. Mae said that she does not care for Brussels sprouts, but she "had neigh-bors, over across the hill, two girls, neither of them never did marry," who loved this vegetable. So, in typical fashion, Mae planted Brussels sprouts for them. She explained, "We were in school together. They didn't have a place for a garden, so I'd always tell them, whatever they want, come over and help themselves. They loved them [Brussels sprouts]. We'd set and visit on the porch. Then they'd pick them. I enjoyed it so much because I'd raise a garden and tell them to come help themselves. And they enjoyed it so much." She paused. "I feed the neighbors."

It could be tempting to see Mae's life as an agrarian romance, but that would be false. She told me point-blank that she dropped out of high school to get married, had three children, and then in midlife had a fourth. That is when her husband left her. And she was nearly fifty when the local physician, Dr. Graves, and Mr. Stevens, who directed the French-burg retirement home where Mae had been working as a nurse's aide, enrolled her in an LPN program in Lexington. She received a scholarship funded by a program to train Appalachian nurses. In those days, nurses mostly trained in the hospital, interspersing classwork with direct

observation and patient care. Her mother, Hannah, who was still alive in the 1960s, took care of Mae's youngest daughter while Mae completed the degree in Lexington. With her training Mae continued to serve the people of Menifee County and made a good-enough living to raise her remaining daughter alone. She also built a house on her twenty acres, the one she lived in when I met her. And she continued to raise a big garden "to make ends meet," as she said.

The garden not only is a source contributing to Mae's physical health and economic well-being but also underpins other dimensions of her life. At least twice, Mae tested prevailing moral authority, with the outcome affecting crops. The first challenge involved her whole family. Usually the Raneys did not grow tobacco on the farm where they were living but did allow those renting one of their farms to do so. But Mae remembered one year that they did grow tobacco. It was a bumper crop. The Raneys, who, following the religious and cultural norms of their community, never worked on Sunday, needed to finish cutting and housing the tobacco before Mr. Raney left home on Monday to begin his week of teaching. They filled the barn and even had to set up temporary scaffolding outside the barn on which to hang the overflow of tobacco.[18] Mae said, "Do you know, what we cut that Sunday—there never was a leaf of it that stayed on the stalk. It got slimy and slick, and instead of curing, slipped off that tobacco stalk. Every bit that we did on Sunday slipped off." Years later Mae staged another test "just to see" whether planting by the signs was a credible system.[19] She had learned how from her mother. "I was right at her heels [whenever she was planting]," Mae said. But once, as an adult, Mae planted her beans at the wrong time, according to the signs. "[They] didn't set on until they were way up the [corn]stalk."

A garden as a site where moral or spiritual actions are mediated and life's lessons are cultivated is likely more rare today than in the world into which Mae was born. Certainly, gardening has skipped a generation in Mae's family. None of her children keeps a garden. But an adult granddaughter does, and Mae has been her teacher. This granddaughter is poised to carry on and adapt Mae's knowledge and practice. And all of us could benefit by infusing Mae's habits into our own: *Take a day of rest, follow the signs, can and dry and pickle.* And though Mae would never say this, I will: *Stay in Mae Raney Sons's light.*

"DA MUCHAS VUELTAS LA VIDA"
(LIFE, IT TAKES A LOT OF TURNS)

Maria and Ciro Prudente

TACKLING NEW SITUATIONS and mastering new skills do not intimidate Maria and Ciro Prudente.[20] Without hesitation, they became the first gardeners to join the Russell County Cooperative Extension's Hispanic Gardening Project.[21] At the time Ciro was supplementing his income from welding at Tarter Gates, a local company that makes farm fencing, by doing agricultural work for Frankie and Brenda Antle. The Antles' daughter, Pam York, county extension agent for family and consumer sciences in Russell County, helped initiate the pilot garden on land donated by the Antle family. York recruited Ciro and Maria; later, Ciro enlisted more gardeners. I asked Maria what about the project piqued their interest. She said, "[We wanted] to learn, to see what it was all about because we had never grown anything. We wanted to learn how to plant the potatoes and the chili peppers—jalapenos, poblanos, bananas." To those vegetables, Maria and Ciro added a considerable repertoire: zucchini, pumpkins, cucumbers, tomatillos, tomatoes, watermelons, cantaloupes, corn, sweet potatoes, cauliflower, lettuce, cilantro, green onions, carrots, and radishes.

Besides relishing fresh food in the summer months, the Prudentes became enthusiastic canners. One of the goals of the Hispanic Gardening

Project was to provide greater access to fresh and healthy food. Preserving summer's bounty so that vegetables can be eaten in the winter is a way to extend the garden's reach. The Russell County Cooperative Extension staff taught the gardeners how to can, freeze, and pickle. Ciro said, "The best thing is you grow your own food, then can it and have it all year long." Maria, who was the person doing the canning, was emphatic about the advantages of food preservation. "What I like best [about the gardening project] is canning," she said, "because I like the kitchen, I like the cooking. And I like [the food] because I canned it." Like many longtime rural Kentuckians, Maria canned tomatoes and froze corn. But true to her own cuisine, she also canned tomatillos and pickled chilis. And Maria experimented with freezing poblanos, a pepper she needs but one that is not readily found in the supermarkets in Russell County.

I wondered what other benefits gardening held for Maria and Ciro, outside of having fresh food and bolstering the family budget. "We learn," Ciro said simply. For Maria, working in the community garden also provided her with a richer social life. As she put it, one of the benefits is "to meet new people." Even though Maria and Ciro were the only gardeners initially, they met the Cooperative Extension staff, and eventually they would meet other Latino gardeners who would join the project, including Marisol Ortiz, a Puerto Rican transplant, who acted as an English-Spanish interpreter.[22]

Gardening can be hot and physically demanding work, but Ciro is undaunted. He has been working since he was ten years old. He was born in 1977 in Acapulco, the largest city in the Mexican state of Guerrero. Once an iconic beach resort for Hollywood stars in the mid-twentieth century, the port city on the Pacific coast also catered to vacationing middle-class Mexicans and foreigners by the time Ciro was a boy. "[I]t took forty-five minutes by bus to get from my [neighborhood on the outskirts] to the town center," Ciro said. "I worked there . . . polishing cars at the stoplights, [and] I would sing on the beach for the tourists." Ciro concluded with a boyish grin, "But I wasn't a good singer."

When Ciro was thirteen, his parents had divorced, and he, his two brothers, and his three sisters were under the sole care of their mother. She earned a living for her family as a seamstress, selling the clothes she made directly from their home. At age fifteen, Ciro began accompanying his mother to Manzanillo in the smaller state of Colima, north of Guerrero. She took her clothes there to sell because the market was stronger for clothing, Ciro said. "In Acapulco, there's a lot of competition." It was a fourteen-hour trip between Acapulco and Manzanillo.

While Ciro helped his mother with her sewing business in Manzanillo, he also found love there. "I was fourteen when we met," Maria said. "My mother raised chickens, rabbits, [and] pigs. We sold eggs and the chickens and rabbits. That's how we lived, how we earned our living." Neither Maria nor Ciro grew up in a household where vegetables were grown, but they both remembered gathering the fruits that grew naturally in their home habitats: coconut, mango, and plantain. In 1997, when Maria was nineteen and Ciro twenty, the couple left Mexico for their first trip to the United States. By then they had a son, Cesar, and they were looking for work opportunities.

The Prudente family first lived in Florida, then eventually moved to Kentucky. At this point during the interview Ciro began to speak in English, perhaps because he was no longer talking about life in Mexico but rather the life he had forged in the United States. "We like it here better than Florida," he said. In Kentucky, they initially lived in Pulaski County in a small community called Nancy. By then, they had a second child, a daughter, Niyeli. "[At first] we cut tobacco, [but] then the lady I was working for got cows. She asked me, did I want to work milking cows? I told her, 'Yes, I will try.' I worked for six months milking cows. But then in wintertime I didn't like it because the house [that was provided] was rough. The house was not so good. The air was coming in. Then I quit milking and came here to Tarter Gates." After less than a year in Kentucky, Ciro had learned how to work tobacco, milk cows, and weld.

During our interview, just before Christmas in 2009, I learned that the Prudentes were expecting another baby, their third child, the following May. I asked if they imagined themselves growing old in Kentucky. Maria responded, "I don't know. Life, it takes a lot of turns. We don't know exactly what we want. We had a house built in Mexico but we're here." Ciro jumped in, "Especially right now, we have family in Mexico." Ciro's mother and other family members now live in Manzanillo, Maria's hometown. He continued, his voice trailing off, "You never know . . ." I tried to make a point for staying in Kentucky and said, "But your garden is here." We laughed together, sharing an understanding of how a garden can tie us to a place. Maria continued, tentatively throwing out more evidence on the side of staying, "We just bought a trailer and we're fixing it up." They began to discuss the workflow of the spring garden, when Maria will be very pregnant. Ciro predicted that she would be able to help with the harvesting but definitely not the planting and weeding.[23] I was encouraged. They were discussing next year's garden while it was still the dead of winter. It was a good sign, but I, too, knew that *da muchas vueltas la vida.*

CAN DO

Rossneau Ealom

ROSSNEAU EALOM probably would not have become a gardener if he had not fallen in love with Loretta Shanklin. He would not have even met his future wife without the intervention of an army buddy and his girlfriend. And then what are the chances that we will find our one true love when we are well into middle age and do not even live in the same state? In so many ways, Rossneau and Loretta could not have been more different, yet they seemed destined for each other. But that is the thing about love and gardening: each requires a combination of tenderness, determination, and a little help from greater forces.

Loretta grew up on a Todd County farm that had been in her family for at least one hundred years, according to Rossneau. The Shanklins were part of an African American settlement of landowners and farmers in the northern section of the county. The Little Union Baptist Church— exactly one mile from Loretta's homeplace—served as a hub for the community.[24] Rossneau's childhood was less rooted. As a boy growing up in the late 1940s and 1950s, he and the younger half of his siblings lived in Paducah with their great-aunt Lula Porter and, at intervals, with their mother. Ms. Porter, whom Rossneau described as not "the youngest person around," gardened at the back of her rented shotgun house in a segregated neighborhood. Rossneau said, "At that time if you had a house with a little property behind it, people grew a garden in whatever they had.

That's what they did. That's how we survived, too, but I never did know what that was about." His only job was to keep the pigeons out of the small garden in which his aunt grew corn, pole beans, tomatoes, onions, beets, and turnip greens. "She didn't want us in her garden."

Though he began his secondary education at Paducah's Lincoln High School, Rossneau finished in Louisville, where he had gone to live with his older sister. He returned to Paducah briefly before a brother came from Cleveland—a city to which many of Rossneau's older siblings had migrated—to get him. "And that's the beginning of a long, sometimes difficult life," Rossneau offered. "I had a difficult life as a child, too. But later on it was a little different because then I was understanding what was going on. No doubt about it. If you were black during that time, it was difficult."

One of the stories that symbolized what it was like to be a young black man in 1962 in Cleveland—and likely many other cities across the United States at the time—Rossneau told in chilling detail. He recalled, "[The incident] really made me look at the reality of who I was and where I was." Fresh out of high school, Rossneau obtained a job painting window frames in a six-story apartment building on Cleveland's white and affluent west side. He said, "I was up on a ladder. I had a gallon bucket of paint and a paintbrush. I was up on the third floor. These kids used to come by every day, and they would mess with the ladder. Shake it with me up there on it and call me all the 'n' names. Boys and girls. I was up on that ladder, and I got so angry. I told them to stop, and they wouldn't stop. I dropped the bucket full of white paint, and it splattered on every one of them. I shimmied down that ladder real fast, and I got out of the neighborhood. They left and ran home. Now, I am a black kid, so I knew what is going to happen to me if someone catches me. I already know this. I mean, I get." Rossneau ran to the car dealership where his brother-in-law worked, which was owned by the same man whose apartment building he had been painting. They protected him.

While his employer and brother-in-law had sheltered Rossneau from physical harm, his mother had provided him with an internal

counternarrative that provided psychological safety and moral equilib-
rium. She had told her children, "If you get into trouble and go to reform
school, Mama won't be there to get you." Rossneau explained the significance: "It reminded me as a young man when I started to do something
[risky] I had a little fellow sitting on my shoulder, and he would kind of
whisper in my ear, 'Remember what Mama said.'" The day he was standing on the ladder, he was unable to heed his mother's admonition, but he
had also been lucky: he had not been pursued either by the authorities or
by the racist young people who had taunted him. That is why when the
army drafted him in October 1962, a few months after the episode and
his eighteenth birthday, Rossneau thought the military was not an altogether unhappy alternative to reform school or worse.

"In the military I liked what I was doing," Rossneau said. "I had a place
to sleep, I had three meals a day. I had all the warm clothing [I needed]. I
could bathe twice or three times a day [if I wanted]. All that stuff I'd
never had. It was a luxury for me and a bunch of us that were there." After
his two-year draft was complete, he enlisted, remaining in the army for
twenty-three years. He traveled in Europe and the United States, and
when he retired in 1985 he was a first sergeant managing the affairs of his
company's soldiers.

During those military years, gardening was certainly not on Rossneau's mind, though he remembered with pleasure the time he partici-
pated in a German community's grape harvest, along with fellow soldiers.
Rossneau had contemplated love, though. As a young draftee he had married, but in his own words, it was a union "doomed to failure." He said, "I
had spent all the rest of this time looking for this woman that I believed I
could trust and I had confidence in. I met Miss Loretta in 1983 over the
telephone. It was a romantic thing." Introduced by his army buddy's girlfriend, they talked by phone for thirty days before they met face to face.
Then they courted for two more years before marrying. "She was what I
was looking for. She was a lovely creature. I just loved her," Rossneau said.
Loretta was a widow who had raised seven children on her family farm

and had completed her bachelor of science degree as well as thirty additional hours toward a master's degree. Rossneau respected that she was "self-supporting" and, as he put it, that their relationship was built on sharing and "mutual caring." Rossneau and Loretta married in 1986 at the Little Union Baptist Church. Afterward they drove the mile to Loretta's farm to begin their married life.

Except for love, Rossneau was not sure why he was back in Kentucky. Workwise, he said, "There was absolutely nothing for me to do." He entered nearby Murray State University to study speech-language pathology, but he grew restless. Eventually he was hired to manage a furniture factory. He had never built furniture or worked in a factory. "But as a military-type manager, I knew how to locate people who knew how to do things," Rossneau explained. In the army he had always been put in charge of something. "I never shirked responsibility." In no time, Rossneau had the factory humming. But one day when he went to work, he learned that the owner had sold the factory. Everyone was told to go home and file for unemployment. Angry and disillusioned that he, the manager, had not been informed ahead of time, he told Loretta, "I ain't working for nobody else." As he cast about for how he might be self-employed, Rossneau accompanied Loretta to the nearby Fairview Vegetable Auction, where she had been buying discounted produce for their table. He noticed that many people there were purchasing in bulk to resell, and that spawned his idea of selling these vegetables at the Hopkinsville Farmers Market. As he and Loretta began their foray into vegetable sales, Rossneau was also discovering his inner gardener and a possible path to self-employment.

Rossneau and Loretta knew they needed help if they were to start growing their own vegetables for market. Loretta had lived on a farm all her life, but her work had never been in the garden. Instead, her domain had been the house, where she either preserved the bounty or cooked it. And Rossneau "had never grown anything in [his] life," following up this admission by saying with emphasis, "I kid you not." He went on, "But I had seen other people grow. I am a concrete person. If I can see you do it, then I can mimic that." In 2001, at a vegetable growing conference offered by the Kentucky Cooperative Extension, Rossneau stood up, introduced himself, and declared, "I'm trying to be a farmer. I don't know anything about farming. I want to grow vegetables. I need somebody to help me." And the help came. From the University of Kentucky, Kentucky State University,[25] and local county extension agents.

While Rossneau had able teachers, some of his most valuable lessons came from his own mistakes. His first garden was too big for a novice, and he recalled that it "didn't work out too well." Plus, he admitted, "I didn't stay here to manage it." Instead, he and Loretta went to New Jersey for her son's wedding right in the middle of the growing season. He returned to a garden "grown up in weeds" and infiltrated by Japanese beetles. He sold what he could but learned that "once you put it in the ground, you got to stay with it."

In the military when Rossneau had been given an assignment, he had never said, "I don't know how to do this." Instead, he recollected, "I'd try and learn how to do it." And besides, he added, "I don't like being told what I can't do. I'll work very hard to prove you wrong." Rossneau applied this lifelong strategy to his new mission: raising vegetables. The next growing season he produced the "biggest, prettiest" tomatoes, bell peppers, watermelons, cantaloupe, squash, and cucumbers. Three factors contributed to this success: Rossneau reduced his plot to a quarter of an acre; a county extension agent came once a week to teach him how to notice and treat problems before they got out of hand; and the Ealoms did not leave home that summer. So after a rough start Rossneau said, "We did real well off each garden that I've raised [since]." As Rossneau became more and more skilled, the Ealoms found they had too much produce—even after farmers' market sales and setting aside for their household. This is when Loretta's training in food preservation reemerged. She and Rossneau took a class from the University of Kentucky's Cooperative Extension on USDA certified canning and began to can everything from turnip greens to pickled okra to green tomato relish. "We had twenty-seven items in our inventory," Rossneau said. Each jar was finished with a personalized label that read, "Loretta's Home Canning." Loretta also baked sweet breads using zucchini and other squash. Producing canned specialty sauces and pickles, as well as freshly baked goods—from vegetables they were already growing—meant they had less waste, had more appeal to a wider range of customers, and were creating what agriculture economists call "value-added" products. Their business plan had come a long way since their initial attempt to resell vegetables bought at auction.

One of the Ealoms' biggest assets was themselves. When they had bought vegetables for resale, they were often unhappy with the quality. So they grew their own vegetables. Rossneau said, "I don't take second-rate vegetables to the market." He aims for "first-rate" produce. When their garden was more bountiful than they had expected, instead of throwing away the excess or selling it at rock-bottom prices, they preserved it and sold it in its new form. When they found themselves up in the wee hours of the morning still canning even though they had to be at the farmers' market at daybreak, they changed their "time management." They were problem solvers extraordinaire. And they loved the sociability of the market. "Loretta and I loved the atmosphere," he mused. And probably most important to their enterprise was their compatibility. "We were a team a long time ago," Rossneau said.

But no amount of ingenuity, hard work, or even sweet love can keep death away. Loretta Shanklin Smith Ealom died on October 3, 2009, at seventy years of age. Rossneau said Loretta was known by the one long plait that fell down her back. She was "very calm, very pleasant, always a smile." And they *always* went to the farmers' market together. When I met Rossneau during the winter of 2009, barely three months after her death, he said, "I don't know how I am going to [go to the market] this year." When I visited again several months later, Rossneau was forging ahead alone. The growing season was under way, and he had found some small pleasure in two new crops—celery and kohlrabi. They looked beautiful and were destined to be his niche crops when he went to market. He knew he would have to educate many of his customers about the kohlrabi and asked me for recipes he could share with them. His garden helped him put one foot in front of the other. Determination will bear fruit in the garden, especially if mixed with a large dose of care. Rossneau had practically been born with determination, and now he had plenty of tender sorrow to bestow upon his crops. And even though greater forces had taken love from him, they might also bring a new season to his garden.

"I DON'T HAVE A MEMORY
THAT'S NOT A GARDEN"

Jennifer Eskew

"IN ALL MY DAYS of looking at gardens, I have never in my life since seen a garden so well tended and weed free," Jennifer Eskew declared, with no hint of boastfulness in her voice as she talked about the garden her family had while she was growing up. "We had probably the biggest garden in the entire holler. Absolutely, we had the most yield." When I wondered why it was the largest garden, she answered, "We were the poorest people in the neighborhood. That's how we ate." The size and productivity of the Eskew family garden was a source of pride, but it was also the corner-stone of their survival and an expression of their community ethic. The neighbor who tilled the garden, the lawyer friend who provided legal services—all requested payment in tomatoes. "Anybody who invested anything in our garden at all," Jennifer recalled, "got a piece of it."

Jennifer was born in 1979 and grew up on the western edge of the city of Ashland in Boyd County. Ashland is an industrial town, head-quarters of Ashland Oil, Armco, and Kentucky Electric Steel. But Jen-nifer's father, trained in the 1970s as an airplane mechanic and machinist in the air force, was unable to find a job when he returned home. "[It was] the Reagan era," Jennifer explained. The early 1980s were marked by a recession and high unemployment. Because of this economic climate,

Jennifer's family moved into the building next door to her father's parents. Their new home had once been an antique store and had no plumbing or central heating. Kerosene heaters, plastic on the windows, and curtains across doorways kept the family warm in winter. Jennifer said, "In the eighties, kids were watching *Transformers* and *Ninja Turtles* on TV, and I had to go to an outhouse."

Running a house, especially one without the conveniences, requires resourcefulness, hard work, and skill. Domestic know-how often comes from family and community mores, passed down through memory from one generation to the next, each editing and adding along the way. Gardening is no different. When Jennifer was only a year old, her grandfather stamped her forever by taking her into the family garden. He had recently had a stroke, so "he had his cane in one hand and me in the other, just packing me around," she said, remembering the story that others have remembered for her. "It has been our garden since my great-grandparents got married."

As a girl Jennifer learned how her family gardened by working alongside her grandmother and parents. Their style was precise, habitual, seasoned, and grand. Rows were laid out with twine and stakes, aided by a yardstick to keep the space between rows equidistant. Crops were placed in the mainly hillside garden, carefully considering the light and shadows of the summer sun in the hollow. I think of Jennifer as a garden biographer, documenting her childhood memories in relation to dirt, rows, furrows, seeds, and plants. No detail lies beyond her memory's grasp. Each vegetable had a past. "Where the cabbage was, it was real wet all the time. And if we didn't pick them in time they would get so big they would start bursting. I've never seen cabbages this big since." The Eskew method for setting out the tomatoes required Jennifer, her father, and mother to work together quickly but gracefully. "We had the rows dug out. My dad usually, or myself when I got older, would go through the rows, and then about every three feet we could take the hoe and dig a bigger hole, almost like a posthole. Usually my mom would go through and drop a tomato plant in that hole. And then I would come by with a bucket full of Miracle-Gro solution. Instead of watering the plant from the top after we planted it, we would take a big thirty-two-ounce cup, like those cheap ones you would get at McDonald's, [and] dump that whole cup on the roots. And that served to break up the dirt on the plant roots from [being compacted in] their little trays they were in and get them nice and wet. I would hold the tomato up. [My dad] would come by with his hoe behind me and plant it real fast before all that water [in the hole] would go away. And we planted the pepper plants and the eggplants the same way, with the hole, the plant, the fertilizer, and then just a very fast burial of the plant up to its first set of leaves. I still do it this way now."

Jennifer remembers the pleasure of those tomatoes when they were ready to be eaten. One of her jobs was to gather the ripe tomatoes and wash them with well water. "There is not a better tomato in the world than one that has been out in the sun, then you put this ice-cold well water on it. It is good. It tasted so good." She shared another memory about summer eating: "In the middle of the table for every dinner was a plate, a big plate of raw vegetables. That was part of your meal every day. And it was the great big tomatoes, usually the size of a small melon, and they were cut in really thick slices. Beside it, you'd have a green pepper that had been cut into strips. Beside that you'd have cucumbers that were peeled and quartered lengthwise into spears. On the other side of the plate was a whole onion, just sliced like a tomato or cut up into wedges. Those fresh vegetables were always the centerpiece of the table. They were colorful, they were pretty, they were well done."

At the time of our interview, Jennifer lived in downtown Lexington, four blocks from Rupp Arena.[26] She said, "The neighborhood I live in is one of the most diverse neighborhoods in all of Lexington—economically, socially, racially. Everybody is up in there. I probably make enough money to live somewhere better, but I'm comfortable here." But it is a hard neighborhood in which to grow vegetables—too much shade, too many buried brick walks and old foundations, too much concrete. Discouraged but not deterred, Jennifer remembered how people at home grew tomatoes in five-gallon buckets, so she replicated that method in her urban garden. And she found that herbs could be tucked into tight spaces with less-than-desirable soil and still thrive. Still, she longs for the big garden of her childhood. "I miss those vegetables. I miss eating fresh. I miss eating with the seasons. I miss my food having flavor. I miss it being readily available because when you wanted something for dinner you'd go outside and pick it."

When I asked Jennifer what her earliest memory of a garden was, she instantly replied, "I don't have a memory that isn't a garden," because every childhood remembrance is intertwined with the patch of earth her family has tended for generations. In her mind, her memory began the day her grandfather carried her into the garden. That was also the moment she was inducted into her family's gardening culture, an ethos Jennifer still embodies. Later, as our conversation came to an end, she mused, "I never thought about the inheritable value of a process before. The way I do things now, the way I treat my scraps, the way I separate my garbage, the way I dig holes, the way I fertilize plants, the way I prune things, the way I cook them, the way I present my meals, [they] all come from how we grew our garden." Jennifer, as an only child, will someday be the only one left in her family to carry on. That a garden holds memory while also shaping it is something she cannot forget.

THE GARDEN OF BEAUTIFUL PERSONS

Marisol Ortiz

SOMETIMES THE GARDENING GENE skips a generation and even crosses the ocean before it reemerges in an unsuspecting progeny in a new place. Consider Marisol Ortiz, who grew up in Ponce, the second-largest city in Puerto Rico. She was born in 1962 to Isabel Rios and Luis D. Ortiz, both of whom were raised in the countryside but never exhibited an interest in growing a garden themselves once they left for Ponce. Every summer, however, Marisol, who was the oldest of seven children, along with the next two oldest sisters, were packed up and taken to stay with their mother's parents for two months. In rural Barrio La Yuca, just north of Ponce, the grandparents had a garden, but the grandchildren were not required to work in it. As Marisol said, with her charming smile, "We were on vacation." Nevertheless, she remembered her grandfather "working really hard in his garden." She said, "It was big. I remember him picking all the [vegetables] and going to the market to sell them." Perhaps that memory was what sparked a passion for gardening that surfaced nearly forty years later when Marisol moved to Jamestown, Kentucky.

The path to Kentucky had its twists and turns. After finishing college, Marisol married her high school sweetheart, Edwin Rosado, who was also her neighbor in Ponce. He was an industrial engineer, and she taught high school science. They had two daughters, Natalie and Roxanne. "All of a sudden [Edwin] lost his job," Marisol said, "and he started to look for something else. We ended up in Texas." When her husband found his new position at the Fruit of the Loom plant near the border at Harlingen, the family began a period of not staying put in any one place for any length of time. They arrived in Texas in 1998, but in 2003 the plant closed, and Fruit of the Loom sent Marisol's husband to the mountains of Rabun County, Georgia. They stayed there for two years until the Clayton plant closed. Then the company sent the family to Jamestown in 2006. Marisol was not looking for a garden, but she was looking for a job and got an interview for an opening at the Russell County Cooperative Extension office. She did not get the job for which she had applied, but she was recruited to translate between Spanish and English for the Cooperative Extension's Hispanic Gardening Project. To be an interpreter for the gardeners, she had to be in the garden with them. So she got a plot, too.

"I wanted to learn how to grow my own vegetables," Marisol said. "I didn't know it was a process. I thought that you just needed to put a seed in the ground, cover it, and water and then you'll have beautiful tomatoes. But that's not the way. I have learned a lot from the people in the extension office. I learned how to start a seed, how to go to the field and plant it, the irrigation system, the fertilizers. When you have to spray you don't use the same [chemical] for every bug." Marisol was also interested in learning how to can and freeze. "I never had the opportunity to see someone doing it. I learned that here," she said. Though in her mind's eye she remembered whole bunches of hanging yellow bananas, orange trees, and berry bushes from her father's homeplace, a coffee farm located near the Toro Negro rain forest in the mountainous center of Puerto Rico— and she misses that cornucopia—in Russell County she turned her attention to growing vegetables that thrive in Kentucky soil. Marisol said, "I love to cook. I decided to plant the things that I most use at my house and the things that you can keep or save—canning and freezing. And the things I like." She cultivates potatoes, tomatoes, corn, summer squash, zucchini, beans, onions, carrots, cabbage, cauliflower, broccoli, eggplants, pumpkins, jalapeños, and bell and cayenne peppers.

Besides learning new skills, Marisol recognizes other benefits of growing her own food. She said, "Number one, it is fresh. It tastes different. I learned that now that I am doing it. Because before, I used to go to the grocery store and get everything. For me, that was fresh. No, it's not. The flavor, you can tell [from the garden produce]. [Second], I am saving money. I am working hard during the summer, but I am saving. I remember last year I just had to go to the grocery store to buy meat because everything else was in my house." Gardening is also "like a therapy," Marisol said. "When you go [to the garden], even though you know it is hard work and it is sunny and it is hot and you have spots on your skin because of the sun, you forget about everything. When I go, I stay there three or four hours, and my daughters start to call me. 'Mom, when are you coming back? We miss you.' [But] they know when it is summer they need to fix their own food because I am working in the garden."

Most gardeners learn the ropes in our families—from parents or grandparents—or we teach ourselves later in life by reading and trial and error, or even by watching YouTube clips. Sometimes if we are lucky we have a neighbor who will show us the way. And in recent years, gardening classes have popped up in communities everywhere. But Marisol came to gardening from a more unusual, but increasingly available, offering: the community garden.[27] Sponsored by Cooperative Extension Services of the University of Kentucky and Kentucky State University, Russell County's Hispanic Gardening Project grew from the understanding that sometimes people do not have enough to eat and that food deserts can exist in rural areas the same as they do in urban neighborhoods.[28] The land for the initial garden was donated in 2008 by farmers Frankie and Brenda Antle, the parents of Pam York, a Russell County extension agent. By the time I visited and interviewed Marisol and some of the other gardeners, the project had expanded onto land, lent by another private owner, adjacent to the extension office and along the main highway in Russell Springs. Though Marisol came into the project because of her language skills, not because she lived in a food desert, she, too, came to appreciate the fresh plenty provided by the garden. Another kind of abundance also grew out of this garden: cross-cultural friendship. The gardeners—there are six to eight families involved in the project at any given time—often work together in the late afternoon and early evening, and naturally they talk. Marisol said, "Oh, we talk about everything. What happened during the week, what we are going to cook. We talk about our countries, because you know some are from Mexico, we are from Puerto Rico, we have one American—Margie.[29] We talk about the kids, the school, the news, the community. And we talk about the family that owns the land [we garden on]: Frankie and Brenda. They are so good. He works all day long because he has tobacco fields, but if we are there, he comes and he helps us. And his wife, too. They are beautiful persons. I've never seen people like that before that help so much the community."

Marisol is herself one of those "beautiful persons" who, without show, works to bring immigrants services that will strengthen the cohesion of the entire community in which they live. She has used her college teacher training in combination with her fluency in Spanish and English in every U.S. town where she has lived. She worked with Hispanic families through the public school system in Harlingen, Texas, while she was mastering English herself. In Clayton, Georgia, she initially stayed at home but then became involved in a summer program for Latino youth focused on discouraging substance use. In Kentucky she became a teacher's assistant for the Head Start program in Russell Springs.[30] And a few weeks after I met Marisol in December 2009 she started a new job with the Lake Cumberland Community Action Agency. Marisol was hired to help build a Head Start program designed specifically for the children of migrant agricultural workers. She was assigned to visit area farmers who hired these workers and to convince both employer and employee to enroll the migrants' children into Head Start. Informally, she had already brought in several more Hispanic families to the gardening project. I asked her whether, in her new capacity, she might recruit more gardeners. She said, "I know in the future they're going to have a waiting list."[31]

Marisol's low-key, steady confidence in the capacity of the community gardening project for building healthier dinner tables, fatter pocketbooks, and stronger communities was convincing. I began to reconsider my gene theory. If a gardening gene actually exists, maybe it is not passed from one person to another but instead is more like a self-seeding flower that crops up and spreads wherever the conditions exist to sustain it. In this case, it took the vision of the Cooperative Extension, the generosity of Frankie and Brenda Antle (who loaned their land for the pilot project), the linguistic talent and mettle of Marisol, and the audacity of novices to work side by side in the Kentucky summer heat, speaking their native tongue and becoming friends and gardeners in their new home.

THE GRACE OF SOIL

Donna and Larry Haire

"I GREW UP with Daddy always being a miner," Donna told me as we sat on the front porch of the Haire home in Crittenden County. Her father, Lafe Linzey, worked in the fluorspar mines. "Crittenden County was the world producer of fluorspar," Donna paused to explain and then continued.[32] "My husband started work in the spar mines but only worked there three months and then went to work in the coal mines. And then my Daddy followed suit when all the spar mines shut down. Now I have two sons in the [coal] mines. We're generations of miners."[33]

But when a day's work was finished underground, the Haire and Linzey families turned to work aboveground, where the sun, rain, and soil rule. Larry grew up on a farm, only two miles down the road from where he and Donna now live. His father worked as a coal miner, in the oil fields, and as a janitor "at the schoolhouse," Larry said. But his calling was as a farmer. Besides vegetables for the household's use, Larry's father grew hay and corn for livestock, including a dozen or so milk cows, on their eighty acres. The Linzeys, too, had a small dairy. Before and after work in the mines, Mr. Linzey milked twenty-four cows, "ran a milk route, [and] made a crop," Donna said proudly. Both families grew vegetables that were more or less common in western Kentucky: green beans, black-eyed peas, okra, summer squash, cucumbers, green onions, radishes, cabbage, and beets. And they raised a few less typical vegetables such as parsnips and peanuts.

They canned and pickled and made sauerkraut. The Linzeys grew sage to season their homemade sausage, and Donna said, "Mama started raising flowers after she got through raising kids."

Donna and Larry, born a year apart—Larry in 1953 and Donna in 1954—have six siblings each. Larry remembers how he, his brothers, and his sisters had to pick up rocks in their garden and fields that were dislodged by his father's spring plowing. Larry also had to "chop" the weeds after being taught by his father how to tell the difference between a nuisance and the early shoots of vegetables.

Donna remembers less about working in the garden, because she did not have to. What she cherishes are the times she got to ride on the truck with her father as he drove his route, picking up milk from the local small dairies and delivering it to a central creamery. She kept the cans organized to account for each dairy's daily tally. She also recalls the lazy days of wading in a cool creek. "My first memories are down on the banks of Livingston Creek, which is a very historical part of our county," Donna said. "We lived on a farm that was a land grant for a Revolutionary War soldier." The farm had been divided up over the years, but the Linzeys owned two parcels of it. The family sold one tract but kept the other when they moved into Marion, the county seat, so their seven children could easily participate in extracurricular activities. The family garden then became a destination—six miles away from home—for the Linzey children, different from Larry's experience, in which the garden was always there, a part of daily life.

Donna's memories reflect this difference. What stands out in her mind is being with her brothers and sisters and father at the farm in the early spring. "Daddy would break the ground with a horse and a one-row plow," Donna said. "We'd take our shoes off and we would walk along behind [the plow]. The soil would be cold and hard. I loved that—the smell of the dirt. Your feet would be tender from having shoes on all winter. Mama probably didn't know that we took our shoes off that early. It would be potato planting time." She continued. "There wasn't anything hard about life then. You wish you could give your children and your grandchildren that . . . to give them that feeling of walking barefoot in the dirt, wading in the creek, [being] with you [as you work]."

Maybe these divergent experiences are what motivated Larry and Donna to maintain separate gardens. Or perhaps they became emboldened to experiment with different methods during their Master Gardener classes taught by the University of Kentucky's Cooperative Extension Service.[34] Larry's garden is massive and linear. According to Donna, "He will plant and plant and plant in huge long rows." Larry admitted that his garden produces "too much for her to handle." Donna leans more toward meandering, small beds interspersed with flowers and herbs. Larry likes to use the rototiller for weed control between rows.

Donna prefers to mulch with leaves and newspapers but will use an herbicide such as Roundup when she feels that the weeds have gotten the best of her. Larry, in contrast, said, "I don't want it around [my plants]." But he is willing to sparingly use the common chemical pesticide Sevin on his potatoes, beans, and corn.

Donna and Larry, however, are simpatico about the direction they are headed. Through their Master Gardener training they have become knowledgeable about the University of Kentucky's research on and protocol for integrated pest management (IPM), which emphasizes a reduction in chemical pesticide use by introducing, for example, biological controls such as beneficial insects. The goal is to control pests, not eradicate them, to maintain a balance at which the plant can continue to thrive: if ladybugs are plentiful, then the aphids' sap-sucking damage will be kept in check. The Haires have particularly focused on increasing the bird population as part of their IPM strategy by cultivating plants that provide food and cover for them. Donna said, "For the most part we do not have a lot of problems with bugs, because of our birds. We encourage more birds, which in turn take care of a lot of the bugs. And we're slowly recognizing that all those bugs are not harmful bugs. [Besides, vegetables] were never meant to be perfect."[35]

Humans are not perfect either, but they are not able to be. This notion is central to the Old Testament creation story staged in the Garden of Eden, in which Adam and Eve's fallibility represents the inherent imperfection of humankind. From the Haires' perspective, gardening is an artifact of this human blemish, but it is also a source of faith. When I asked Donna and Larry why they grew a garden, Larry answered, "It tastes better. And the joy of it." Then he laughed and said, "If I wasn't doing this, I might be in some kind of trouble." Donna joined in the laughter but became more contemplative. "[Gardening] is something that you do because I think we are made from soil. We were made from the dust of the earth and we were put in a garden and told to tend it. And even after the fall when we were cast out of it, a lot of people

say our punishment now is that we have to live by the sweat of our brow. But, to me, that was the hope that was give to us. You can plant something and it is going to grow [if you tend it]. That is what we are supposed to do."

The theological imperative that infuses the Haires' gardening is coupled with something Donna called "connection." She explained, "I'm just saying that there has to be the spiritual connection, that man was meant to have a spiritual connection with the soil, apart from the physical and emotional benefits that you get [from a vegetable garden]." The sacred bond between humans and the soil is not meant to be solely a private, introspective condition, according to Donna: your garden should be visible to others because gardens build community. Put another way, people see what you are doing, and you see them looking. Recognition. A connection has been made from which understanding and cooperation might emerge.

The Haires' work with children through 4-H is perhaps a more tangible demonstration of a garden's power to bring people together. 4-H (Head, Heart, Hands, and Health) is the youth arm of the Cooperative Extension System, part of the U.S. Department of Agriculture. It aims to develop young people's capacity for building and strengthening the communities in which they live. Larry and Donna work closely with Crittenden County 4-H-ers. "We like to take the opportunity to share with children and make [gardening] exciting or different for them," Donna said. They have taught kids how to plant and decorate gourds, for example. A more elaborate project involved making a "salsa" truck in which all the ingredients necessary were planted in the back of an abandoned pickup truck. The children learned how to make their own potting soil as well as how to tend peppers, tomatoes, and onions. The ultimate lesson was how little space it takes to make a garden that you can eat from. Future teaching projects include how to make sorghum, a particular interest of Larry's, and how to cultivate sweet potatoes.

The Haires call all of this—their Master Gardener certification, 4-H contributions, and extensive home gardens—a hobby. But I disagree. What they do is not a diversion or a mere pastime. It is more like a passionate calling. And Donna attributes it with saving Larry's life and rescuing her from what had been onerous solo work. She said, "If Larry hadn't had to take an early retirement [because of an accident] from the coal mines, I'd still just be out [in the garden] trying to battle it all by myself. I think the garden helped him heal from all of that—emotionally. You've got to have something to give yourself fulfillment. I'm really grateful that we had that to fall back on."

If gardening can supply food for the table, invoke a memory of freshly turned soil on bare feet, provide spiritual and theological continuity, inspire new learning and teaching venues, create stronger communities, heal a spirit flagging from a mining accident, and impart a sense of personal satisfaction, then it is more than a hobby. It is a saving grace.

ARVILLA

Aaron Mansfield

AS A METHODIST MINISTER, Aaron Mansfield knows that part of his job is inviting people to worship. In 2000 when he received his first pastoral assignment—Dunaway United Methodist in the Clark County community of Trapp—he was to learn that just because someone ignores the preacher's knock does not mean that a door has not opened. While going from house to house in his new neighborhood asking people to come to church, Aaron approached one home where he could see a woman inside ignoring his presence. Aaron accepted her rebuff, understanding that in some way he was "invading [her] privacy," as he put it. "[But] about a week later," he recalled, "I'm down at the country store, Fox's Country Store. And this [same] woman comes up to me and said, 'Are you that new Methodist preacher?' And I said, 'Well, sure.' And we got to talking." Her name was Arvilla. "'If I bring you some garden food, will you make sure it gets to people who need it? Hungry people who need it?' she asked." Aaron readily agreed, because he imagined she would bring a sack or two of tomatoes to distribute. "Oh, my goodness! She came over with a minivan loaded with cabbages and peppers and a bunch of [different] kinds of tomatoes, onions."

Once Arvilla started coming twice a week with her bounty, Aaron knew, as an individual, he could not keep up with her pace. He asked,

"Arvilla, what are we going to do?" In answer, they started the Clark County Food Security Coalition with the help of multiple churches, the local U.S. Department of Agriculture office, and community services. Even the *Winchester Sun* contributed by publishing "Plant a Row for the Hungry." Though Aaron was a vegetable gardener and the grandson of farmers, he had not considered that growing a garden to feed the hungry could be a ministry. Arvilla had shown him a way to think differently—as a gardener and as a pastor.

Aaron grew up with a father in the air force, so the family moved often. But his father's family had lived and farmed in the Salinas Valley since California was annexed by the United States in the mid-nineteenth century. And his mother's people, while more recent immigrants, had also been longtime farmers in central California. Aaron spent most of his boyhood summers with his grandparents on their farms in the valley. And Aaron's father taught him to plant something wherever he lived, especially trees, because they last and because "you should leave a place better than what you found it." Aaron was primed to be a caretaker of land even if his boyhood experience was to never stay in one place for long. In 1988 he graduated from high school in Biloxi, Mississippi, where his father had been stationed. Aaron told his parents he was not moving again. He entered the nearby University of Southern Mississippi at Hattiesburg and "started gardening in depth," he said. "That's when I had my first big garden that was more than just a few tomatoes. A man I worked for lived outside of town, and he let me have a big garden space."

When Aaron arrived to study literature at the University of Kentucky in the late 1990s, he was reduced to growing in pots on the balcony of a student apartment. Eventually his call to the ministry led him away from graduate school and into the seminary. To support himself, Aaron took a construction job. Again, a boss who owned ten acres in rural Woodford County allowed Aaron to plant a large garden there. "I went hog wild," Aaron said. By the time he met Arvilla in 2000, Aaron was a seasoned gardener but an inexperienced minister. He said, "I never would have thought that growing peas and carrots and tomatoes in my own first garden was going to lead to [a ministry]." But one of the jobs of a pastor, according to Aaron, is to "shut up" and "hang out." When Aaron heeded his own advice, Arvilla came to him with a vision and a minivan load of vegetables.

As a gardener, Aaron describes himself as "cheap" and "lazy," but I think, like Buddhists, he is open to outcome. One summer when he was gone for a week he returned to a garden "overgrown with weeds." He said, "It was going to be too much to kill all the weeds or tear them out, [so] I just mowed them. The next thing I knew, we hit a drought. My stuff was growing fine. And you could see the grass that was growing [between the rows] was holding the moisture in. So the next year I sowed clover straight into the garden and mowed [it] maybe three times that summer. It kept weeds down, added nitrogen back. Then I threw [the grass clippings] on my compost heap." This is Aaron's gardening formula: "[I] put it in the ground and it is going to grow and if something comes out of it, praise God. If something doesn't, maybe I'll figure out why [but] most of my life is 'let's see what happens.'"

At times, though, Aaron bargains with his Lord about pillagers and pests in the garden. When he had his own large garden in Clark County, people warned him that the deer and rabbits would devastate his crops. Aaron resisted this pessimistic outlook. He had his own plan. "I'll just make a deal with the Lord to let me keep some of it," he thought. "It's not so much for me as it is for anybody that is hungry. Let's give it to them." Aaron believed there was enough for everybody: the deer, the rabbits, the hungry in his county, and his loved ones.

In 2006 when Aaron was moved to Lexington, he had to cope with occasional garden marauders of the human species, but his "let's see what happens" spirit created one of the most talked-about community gardens in the city. Assigned to La Roca/The Rock Methodist Church on Lexington's north side, Aaron's new neighborhood was home to established African American and white Appalachian working-class families who had been more recently joined by African refugees and Latino immigrants. French and Spanish and English were spoken, and services at the church reflected these language traditions. As he walked his neighborhood, he noticed that the small grocery stores scattered about were not selling much that might be called healthy. He saw people who likely were hungry. The need for fresh and inexpensive vegetables—the need for food, period—was as great in this neighborhood as it had been in rural Clark County. Arvilla had taught Aaron well: he wanted La Roca to start a garden.

Aaron's new church sat across the street from Arlington Elementary. Behind the school was a good-sized piece of unused land. Aaron asked whether his congregation could use it for a vegetable garden, and the school board agreed. Eventually it grew to four thousand square feet worked by Aaron, the Cuban assistant pastor, several young men who attended the Hispanic service, youths who consistently showed up for four hours on Saturdays, a "neighbor lady," and, "a guy" across the street who provided water. The church used what the garden produced to prepare a weekly "fellowship meal" and to include in food boxes sent home with those who came to the worship supper.

I met Aaron in the spring of 2009 soon after La Roca/The Rock had lost its garden space because the school was scheduled for renovation and expansion. But the wealthy downtown Methodist church intervened by loaning a tract of land it owned on the edge of the city. Already eighteen thousand square feet had been plowed for planting. The garden could continue, but in a location seven miles away from where most of the gardeners lived.

The "let's see what happens" Aaron strategized about how he would transport people out to tend this ambitiously sized garden. But the gardeners were ready. The homemade greenhouse behind the church was brimming with tomato, pepper, and eggplant seedlings. The gardeners aimed to plant various kinds of potatoes, and Aaron's wife, Jessie, intended to grow a sweet potato variety that went back "six or seven generations" in her Illinois family. Some of their crops were to be planted next to the church around the top edge of a large retention basin. People walking on the sidewalk could pick a few beans as they passed by if they wanted. The goal was to raise enough to dispense food to those who came to the weekly fellowship meals but also "to raise money to continue that ministry" by starting a subscription service for local restaurants who would buy produce from the community garden. Aaron explained, "This is a poor church. We're always scraping by."

Even with these challenges Aaron seemed optimistically contemplative. "I'll be interested to see what happens. Where do we go? Where are we in five years? [Will we be] any closer to what is that very distinctively Methodist goal: minister to people's needs, then you start to do it with them because they know better than you do what they need. And then they take over the leadership. They take on the path and you move on your way because now they're doing your job."

Then the bargaining Aaron emerged. "I hope we get to break the Methodist cycle and I get to stay here six or seven more years. It's going to take that long, I think, to see something happen. [But] Methodist ministers—you can't escape it—they move a lot." Connecting his childhood spent as the son of a career military father to the historically itinerant life of a Methodist pastor, Aaron mused, "On the one hand, moving around as a child so much, I can't really avoid moving around as an adult. It just keeps happening. But at the same time I'm trying to find a place where I can just stay. The garden is a motif: even though I may not be staying in one place, it's about as rooted as I get. So everywhere I've gone, [I've] put in a garden."

The inevitable happened in June 2011, as gardening season was fully under way: Aaron was moved to a church in Morehead, a university town about an hour east of Lexington in the Appalachian hills. In a more recent conversation about his new church and his reflections on La Roca, Aaron told me that after he left, the garden project "withered on the vine," in part because the new leadership saw other church undertakings as more pressing. But Aaron speculated about a convergence of other issues that may have undermined the viability of the garden. "I really want to think it was sustainable without me, because if not, then I failed at a critical piece. I also wonder if the people we were working with and serving are often on the move, and so maybe some things can't keep going indefinitely. And the neighborhood [was gentrifying]. I was not really interested in how it looked or it being a community garden in the sense that individuals had a plot. It was meant to grow as much food in its space to feed as many people as possible. It was meant to be worked communally. It had some glorious moments where it grew a lot of food and whites, African refugees, Hispanics, African Americans, young and old were in it and fellowshipping."

La Roca's gardening spirit was well known across Lexington. Aaron and the other gardeners raised awareness about community gardening and its benefits to the city. Churches, community organizations, and plenty of nonbelievers supported the La Roca garden with labor and other contributions. Its absence leaves a hole. And how are the people who were once fed by this garden now making ends meet, nutritionally and spiritually?

I believe there is reason to hope. What Aaron calls *fellowshipping* may be key. When Arvilla approached Aaron, then a newly ordained pastor, with her need to distribute "garden food" to the hungry, she was seeking fellowship. Aaron, taking his cue from Arvilla, helped create a context for fellowship at La Roca, in a communally worked garden that fed body and spirit. That garden may have "withered," but surely a few new Arvillas germinated there. Sustainability resides in the design of the project but also in those who give the plan its shape and rhythm. Some year when spring is coming, former La Roca gardeners will be found somewhere planting vegetables for those who need a fresh bite because sustainable fellowship needs both the garden and the gardener.

DIVINE LAND

Mattie and Bill Mack

A HINT OF FALL was in the air when I arrived midmorning on a late September day at the Macks' Meade County farm. To get there I had crossed the Ohio River twice—once at Louisville into Indiana and then again as I turned southward back into Kentucky. The Macks live in a stone 1970s ranch-style house on a one-hundred-acre working farm complete with cattle, tobacco, and white board fencing along the road frontage. Miss Mattie was waiting for me at the front door.

As I listened to Miss Mattie's stories about her childhood, I had difficulty imagining why she had chosen a life of farming and gardening. Born in Fayetteville, Georgia, in 1937 near the end of the Great Depression, she was one of eleven children, including two sets of twins. Miss Mattie was herself a twin. During the growing season, the children worked on their father's mother's farm, where cotton, greens, and sweet potatoes were grown. By age eleven, "Little Sister"—that's Miss Mattie—and her twin, "Big Sister," were already learning to plow with mules. At this tender age Miss Mattie also experienced the power a mule could have over the uninitiated. "A snake was going across the field, and Old Kate got excited," she said. "She jumped up, reared up, and took off. Well, my hand that was 'round that lead—on the right hand you say 'gee' and the other hand you say 'haw'—it came off, and I stepped to get it and my foot hung up in that rope and it tightened. [Old Kate] pulled me all over the field. I was screaming and hollering." The next day her foot was so swollen that her mother put her in the wagon and took her to see Dr. Sams. "In those days," Miss Mattie said frankly, "you had to go to the doctor in the back."[36] No bones were broken, but the doctor did give her a shot, and with rest she eventually got better. "I never did get to plow anymore, and I didn't cry about it either."

Miss Mattie is nothing if not forthright. "We had a rough time," she remembered. She described the house in which she grew up as a "shack" with dirt floors and no nearby water source. There was no spare ground to make a garden. She told me that she realized in adulthood that "people put coal in those kind of houses like we lived in." Her father "was a poor provider" who loved women and abused alcohol. Miss Julia, "a white lady with a bunch of chickens," gave Miss Mattie's mother, Roxie, feed sacks that she would transform into dresses for her daughters, one "to go to school and one to go to church." The children were not always able to attend school, because they had to chop and pick cotton, but this hard work may have precipitated the questions Miss Mattie and her siblings began to ask about their conditions. Why were they working for their father and grandmother, who did not pay them or even feed them well while they were working? Why was their mother, whom they loved dearly, unable to buy enough food? "Mama," they asked, "if we big enough and old enough to pick Grandma's cotton, why can't we catch those migrant trucks and go and make some money?" "Migrant trucks" came around to pick up people for day labor in the fields. Miss Mattie described seven or eight trucks "full of folks" driving out to cotton fields owned by "rich white people." She went on to explain the significance of this paid labor. "Mama had four in the field, and we hoed the cotton for three dollars a day. So Mama had quite a bit of money. [She] would give us a quarter of the money, and she would buy food [with the rest]." This new infusion of cash also brought new experiences. Relishing the memory of her first sandwich with store-bought sliced bread, "sandwich spread," and bologna, Miss Mattie said, "We thought we were in heaven."

Miss Mattie's life is like a dance between hard times with a not-so-small dose of evil mixed in and what even a skeptic like me might call divine intervention. Miss Mattie's path to the Tuskegee Institute illustrates mightily this dance. [37] Around the age of fourteen she quit working on the "migrant trucks" and began doing housework for a white woman, Miss Trimble, who was a skilled seamstress. Mr. Trimble owned a lumberyard. They had an adopted daughter named Nancy whom Miss Mattie declared a "real Gypsy." Miss Mattie told me that Miss Trimble was "crazy" about her. "She would fix me lunch." Miss Trimble bragged on the quality of Miss Mattie's work by telling her, "I love the way you work. You're a real good worker." For an afternoon of labor, she paid Miss Mattie three dollars and would then "run her home." Miss Trimble would often send Miss Mattie home with Nancy's older dresses, too. "I was tickled to death," she freely revealed. Miss Mattie liked the Trimbles but was very conscious of one forbidden closet in their home: "Don't ever open that," Miss Trimble warned her as she locked the door with a skeleton key.

As the locked closet piqued Miss Mattie's curiosity, serious terrors marched into her life: the Ku Klux Klan. Her community had its own town crier—a young man who rode a bicycle down the dirt roads, bouncing and rattling from one hole to another, yelling, "They're coming, they're coming!" With this warning, all nearby African Americans "would run to the hills." Speaking softly, Miss Mattie recalled how her community hid together in the countryside. In particular, Miss Mattie remembered the time when her family returned to see the obligatory cross burning in front of their home. Her mother put what was left in the stove to burn, telling her children, "Don't never think about it," and then turned to help them get ready for school.

Sometimes a trauma is best denied in the moment, but its erasure will never be complete. The shock may grip us later. One day while cleaning at the Trimbles—Miss Trimble was in Atlanta buying fabric for her dressmaking business—Miss Mattie decided she had to know what was in the locked closet. She had seen where Miss Trimble kept the key. "I opened the door," she told me in a shaky voice, "and there was those hoods, those sheets. And I stood there and I trembled. I couldn't move, I was so numb. When I could, I ran out. I ran home, I ran all the way." Miss Mattie's mother demanded to know what was wrong. But Miss Mattie was unable to talk, so her mother threw water in her face and then dried her off. Finally Miss Mattie said, "Miss Trimble is one of them." "One of what?" her mother asked. "The Ku Klux Klan." Miss Mattie was nearly whispering at this point in her story. She took a breath and continued a little louder. "Then that afternoon here came Miss Trimble and Mr. Trimble." Miss Trimble said to Miss Mattie's mother, who had gone to the door, "Where is Little Sister?" "She's in the house, Miss Trimble. She ain't coming back there no more." But Miss Trimble insisted. Miss Mattie came to the door. "I want you to listen," Miss Trimble said kindly to Miss Mattie and her mother. "We have to wear those hoods. We have to wear those sheets. Because if they don't see us in these, you know what they would do? They would burn up his timber." Mr. Trimble then spoke. "We don't have nothing against y'all. You know I love you, Little Sister. But we had to do what they said to do." Miss Trimble asked whether she would come back to work for them. Miss Mattie told her mother, "I love Miss Trimble and Nancy. Mama, they're good people. They treat me so good. I've never been treated like this before." Her mother relented. When Miss Mattie graduated from high school, Mr. Trimble gave her money and Miss Trimble gave her clothes. With these resources added to what her mother had been saving, Miss Mattie made her way to Tuskegee Institute to study nursing.

"I was so dumb and green," Miss Mattie recalled. She thought a doctor brought a new baby in a "big black bag" because that is what her mother had told her. She fainted when she observed her first birth as part of her studies. Socially, she was inclined to retreat, to not take chances. Miss Coleman, a nurse and teacher, intervened. Was it divine? I am not sure, but Miss Coleman's guidance certainly influenced the course of Miss Mattie's life. Miss Coleman took Miss Mattie out to eat one evening—her first meal in a restaurant. Also in the cafe that evening was Kentuckian Bill Mack, a veterinary science student at Tuskegee. Later he called to ask Miss Mattie to a dance. She wanted to decline. "We was taught not to dance, that's the devil's dance," she told Miss Coleman. But her teacher said firmly, "No, you haven't been anywhere. You're going." Then Miss Mattie protested that she had nothing to wear. Miss Coleman marched to her room and picked out one of Nancy Trimble's old dresses. She began to take it apart, reimagine its style. Working quickly, "she began to pull the sleeves out. She took the collar off. And she reworked it." After adding one of her own red ribbons to the dress, now no longer a Nancy hand-me-down but an original design, Miss Coleman fixed Miss Mattie's hair in a "poodle," a style that boasts curls all over the head. As Miss Mattie descended from the third floor of her dormitory to the parlor, Mr. Mack stood at the bottom of the steps. "You look beautiful," he told her. Miss Mattie questioned such a compliment: "I do?" "You sure do," he reassured her. With that first date Miss Mattie's trajectory to becoming a Kentuckian and a gardener began.

Maybe the Macks would have moved to Kentucky anyway. Mr. Mack grew up in Shelby County, around the community of Montclair, and attended the Lincoln Institute at nearby Simpsonville.[38] His parents were sharecroppers who helped their son attend Kentucky State to study agriculture. From there he was sent to Tuskegee. He never quite finished his veterinary studies there because of something that happened the night after he and Miss Mattie got married. They were stopped by the Fayetteville, Georgia, police for having a string of tin cans tied to the back fender as they drove through town, announcing "Just Married." This common practice of blacks and whites—at least in the South of the time—signals and celebrates that a marriage has taken place, that the couple in the car are newlyweds. The police ordered them to remove the cans, and when the Macks objected to the blatant unfairness, the police yelled racial slurs and threatened to jail them. After untying the cans, Mr. Mack got back in the car and said, "We're going to get out of here." The next morning they got on a train bound for Louisville.

The Macks were young, capable people who were willing to work hard, and they did. They managed a dairy farm for five years in Breckinridge County and then lived in a one-room apartment on East Chestnut in Louisville while Miss Mattie worked as an LPN at Children's Hospital in the ER and Mr. Mack inspected restaurants for the health department by day and waited tables at the Brown Suburban and Brown Hotels by night. "I always worked two or three jobs all my life, to try to get something," Mr. Mack offered. "Back then, black men made a fortune waiting tables. You could make a killing." Mr. Mack would even leave home some summers to work in Michigan at a resort hotel on Mackinac Island in Lake Huron. He told me, "I went up there three years straight. It was seasonal work. I would come back and put my money in the bank." In these early years of their marriage, all their hard work was galvanized by their dream, the dream of owning their own land.

Initially, they wanted to buy a farm in Jefferson County, where Louisville is located, but in the early 1960s that was a near impossibility for an

African American. Mr. Mack put it this way: "There was prejudice." Then he elaborated. "In 1962, they wouldn't sell to a black person. Everywhere we went in Jefferson County was owned by whites. Whew! We went to some of those white farms, and they were going to sic their dogs on us. [They'd say to us,] 'Y'all get out of here. We don't sell to no blacks.' We jumped in the car and took off."

Then divine intervention occurred: the Macks met a real estate agent who could help them. Miss Jarboe "wasn't all white, she was mixed." And she knew about a farm in Meade County for sale, owned by an African American, Mr. James L. Bell. He worked for Mammoth Life and Accident Insurance Company, a Louisville-based firm owned by African Americans. "He was a big shot with black people," Mr. Mack said admiringly. "Blacks would borrow money from him. He had money. He was big time." Mr. Mack continued. "As soon as we turned in, Mattie said, 'I ain't going no further. This is the farm we are going to buy.'" When the young Mattie and Bill told Mr. Bell they had "come to buy this farm," he said, "Y'all don't have no money. Y'all kids. I want ten thousand dollars down and two thousand dollars a year for this farm. I've got a white guy up in Valley Station who's going to buy this farm. He's got to sell his house first." Mr. Mack then politely responded, "Well, Mr. Bell, you give us a week and we'll come back with your money." A week passed and the Macks returned with ten thousand dollars to buy the hundred-acre farm. "He couldn't believe it," Mr. Mack said, relishing the memory. "The next week after that, the white guy sold his farm at Valley Station. The Lord is good."[39]

About eight years later while Miss Mattie was at church and Mr. Mack was out cutting firewood, the original white two-story house was destroyed by a fire. Mr. Bell financed the building of the stone ranch house where the Macks still live.[40] There they finished raising their four children and thirty-eight foster children. Mr. Mack put in thirty years at Olin Chemical in Brandenburg, the county seat, while he farmed. Miss Mattie farmed, kept a big garden, and put up food. When I asked them to

reflect on their life as gardeners and farmers, Mr. Mack, then seventy-seven years old, talked about the freedom farming allows. "It's independent. The farmer never will quit. They come and go. You can't tell them what to do." He concluded with deep satisfaction, "I wouldn't take nothing for [my life]. I'm not going nowhere." Hearing this, Miss Mattie got back in the conversation and reaffirmed, "I'm not going nowhere neither." Maybe this is how divine intervention actually works: if you are lucky, it takes you to a place you never want to leave.

A MOTHER'S BEANS

Tom Collins

"I AM A HILLBILLY from eastern Kentucky," Tom told me when we first met, laughing but gently defiant. "My family is from Breathitt County. I grew up very poor in a huge family. I'm lucky number thirteen out of fourteen children." His directness appealed to me.

"Where in Breathitt County?" I asked.

"The tiny little community of Barwick."

I remembered that Barwick was one of Robert Kennedy's stops on his 1968 tour of eastern Kentucky, just months before his assassination. Tom, born two years before, in 1966, could not recall Kennedy's visit. But in one of his family's photo albums is a picture of his sister Melinda with the senator when he had visited Barwick's one-room school. Kennedy had gone to eastern Kentucky to investigate the effects of the War on Poverty, the social and economic programs first imagined during John Kennedy's administration and realized during Lyndon Johnson's. Tom entered first grade in that same school a few years later.

By then he was already working in what he calls "a feed-your-family garden." One of his earliest garden memories is of his mother and older brothers and sisters working as he sat in the grass at the garden's edge. He remembers listening to his siblings "complaining and crying and wanting to get out of the garden" as he watched them hoe. Soon, Tom himself was old enough to pull weeds and be tutored by his mother in garden ways. The garden was her domain.

"The major lesson I learned from my parents was self-sufficiency, that you have to be able to take care of yourself," Tom said. "I saw that everything [my mother] was doing was a lesson [in] how you take care of yourself." Her garden was carefully calculated to be productive seven or eight months out of the year. "The first things that would go in in the spring would be Black-Seeded Simpson lettuce, mustard greens, onions, and sweet peas," followed shortly by Irish Cobbler and Kennebec potatoes. "We would have tons and tons of cabbage. Cabbage meant sauerkraut." Then came other garden staples, such as tomatoes, corn, and green beans. The latter were often planted where the lettuces had grown a month earlier. At summer's end when the onions were "lifted," the Collins family would plant a second crop of cucumbers to get a last stand before frost. Once the potatoes were dug, they would immediately sow "seeds for mustard greens and turnips. And the turnips would grow right into the winter," Tom recalled. "I can remember snow being on the turnip tops." The term for this efficiency of scale, Tom told me, is "double-cropping."

The family's subsistence relied on more than a vegetable garden. They raised soybeans and corn to provide feed for their milk cows, pigs, and chickens. But not one to waste a space where food could grow, Tom's mother planted vining pumpkins, gourds, and cushaws to crawl through the corn patches.[41] "It was magical walking through the cornfields," Tom said. Marveling, he remembered "the shapes, the textures . . . and the colors" of his mother's design. What was unusual about Tom's family, given that they had such a large and productive enterprise, was that they owned hardly any land: only the house and about an acre around it. Otherwise, the land they cultivated was owned by the Pine Branch Coal Company, for whom Tom's father had long worked. Some "large river bottoms," the richest land, belonged to extended family. Without this borrowed land, the Collins family livelihood would have been sparse and extra money for academic pursuits likely impossible to raise. "My mom would have a roadside stand and

sell sweet corn to give me the money to buy textbooks" for college, said Tom, who also picked wild blackberries, a hot and prickly job, to earn money for school clothes.

Tom remembers conversations around the supper table during which the family imagined, as many families did during those years, who would survive if nuclear warfare ever took place. They reasoned, "If any part of civilization will ever survive, it will be in eastern Kentucky or similar places, where people actually did save seeds and where they saved, along with the seeds, the stories of how to work the soil." For the Collinses, one of the crucial seeds would be the "little creamy bean." Passed down through the family, the seed embodies their theory and practice of self-sufficiency.

"My mom got her creamy beans from her mom, who got hers from her mom. Little creamy beans. It's a bunch bean.[42] The beans are very short. They only grow just three or four inches long. And each pod will only have five or six beans to it, but the bean itself [gets] really big." When cooked, the little creamy bean has a "meaty pork-like flavor," Tom explained in a reverential tone. As the bean begins to cool, though, "it goes from green to sort of a blackish color." To the uninitiated, "it doesn't look appetizing."

I wondered how Tom got the little creamy-bean seed when generally it is "passed down from mother to daughter when a daughter gets married." Tom's mother, however, did not have a daughter to pass the beans on to, because Tom's eight sisters, all older, have not carried on the tradition of gardening as he has. When Tom and his partner, Michael, started a household together, Tom asked for a "jar full of seeds" for his first garden at his new Lexington home. His mother, breaking tradition in order to maintain it, passed the little creamy-bean seeds on to Tom.

Michael, who had never eaten fresh green beans before Tom came into his life, now manifests a passion that all converts seem to have. Tom, laughing, recalled, "When Michael first saw these green beans I think he was disgusted. He said, 'They're not green; they're *not* green.' But now he tells me, 'Make sure that you plant some of the little creamy beans. And when you can, make sure you mark those and can those for us. Don't give them away.'"

Before our evening ended, Tom took me out back to show me his pet chickens, stopping to put on his "yard shoes" just as I imagined his mother taught him to do. He has a coop near his small garden plot with Bantam Silkies, a small ornamental breed. He told me that at his nephew's place in nearby Bourbon County he keeps a flock of laying hens—Barred and White Rocks, Rhode Island Reds, New Hampshires, Comets, Jersey Black Giants, and Easter Eggers. There, he also has a large "feed-your-family garden." I realized then that Tom was replicating, with some adjustments, his mother's eastern Kentucky domain. He sent me home with canned goods, including a signature tomato sauce, but, sadly, no creamy beans. As I left, I could see Tom turning to clean up the kitchen from the big meal he had prepared for Michael and me. I remembered how lovingly he talked about his closeness with his mother throughout our interview: "When you're one of fourteen, it is hard to stand out. The gardening allowed me to distinguish myself from my brothers and sisters. It was something special I had with my mom." Although I did not meet Mrs. Collins that night, I knew that all the weight of her knowledge, skills, and generous spirit had made the evening possible. She had taught Tom how to take care of himself and his family and how to treat company.

If only everyone had a good teacher, a good bean, and the willingness to reimagine tradition.

LIVE SIMPLY

Janice Musick

ONE SUNDAY MORNING in early April, I drove to Whitley County to meet Janice Musick. It was a perfect spring day in Kentucky: crisp but warming air, cottony clouds fast-forwarding across a blue sky, the smell of dirt rising up, creeks running full but clear, and the woods coming alive, dressed in a pale green outline of budding leaves. If you thought you would die before winter was over, this was the kind of day that would make you glad you stuck it out.

As I drove up Jellico Creek, I could see the first of the three garden plots Janice tends in the narrow bottom of her hillside homestead. Then I saw Janice huddled over a row, swiftly planting onions. A young woman and man were helping in adjacent rows. They all looked up and waved— the way people do in the country when not many cars pass by—but continued with their work. I drove on past, up to the house, and waited. In due time the three arrived by truck. Janice had told me to arrive at 1:00, but I was a bit early. We were going to conduct the interview over lunch, and then the gardeners would return to their planting. Janice, an inveterate home gardener now in middle age, had decided to begin selling produce in nearby Tennessee at the Knoxville farmers' market and to start a small community-supported agriculture (CSA) project, an agreement between a grower and a household to subscribe for a season at a prepaid price for a supply of fresh produce. She needed to plant more than usual.

This is Janice's economy and guidepost: live simply, grow organically, and work hard. But the idea of maneuvering and surviving within an alternative economy is nothing new for Janice. In the early 1970s, after she dropped out of college, she was, in her words, a "hippie" and "back-to-the-lander." Living outside of Athens, Ohio, she bartered her services—cooking, gardening, and putting up food—and in return, friends gave her a place to stay. She also landed on Prince Edward Island in Canada for a period, with friends who were dodging the draft for the Vietnam War. She said, "It was really fun for me there because there was no electricity. [T]hey were cooking on a wood-burning cookstove, they were growing a garden, they were canning. They had a milk cow. So I taught them stuff I had learned on the farm: how to make cottage cheese and butter. They taught me how to bake bread in a wood-burning cookstove."

Later, Baltimore attracted Janice, because she wanted to study macrobiotics at a center there. Like many other young people at the time, Janice was seeking alternatives to corporately produced and processed food and was searching for new forms of spirituality. Macrobiotics is both a way of eating and a philosophical and spiritual practice that borrows from Zen Buddhism. The diet is primarily vegetarian and relies chiefly on whole grains and seasonal, local fruits and vegetables. Once in Baltimore she met people who were macrobiotic; she rented a room from them and "got to learn a lot hands-on, helping prepare [their] meals." She also made meals for evening lectures at the center so that she could attend for free.

Hands-on learning runs deep in Janice's life. She grew up on a nine-acre farm near Akron, Ohio. Her father worked in a machine shop and her mother as a nurse, on the weekend. But during the week Janice's mother, who was raised on an Ohio farm, ran what Janice called their "self-sufficient farm," which included a large garden. They canned and froze their produce, milked a cow, raised a hog to butcher, grew corn and hay to feed the animals, and kept fruit trees. Janice told me, "I loved it. My brother and I, we mostly ate what we grew."

Janice's parents met during World War II in the army. Her father, a Kentucky native, was a sergeant on a ship transporting wounded soldiers, and her mother, a lieutenant, was stationed in England as a nurse. After the war, they married and settled on his family's Whitley County farm while Mr. Musick taught in the public school at Williamsburg, the county seat. Janice's mother fell in love with the Kentucky mountains. But by the time Janice was born in 1953 they had moved to Ohio. Like many other eastern Kentuckians of their generation, they migrated to find more lucrative work. When Janice was nineteen years old, her father died. Her mother

bought a trailer for the Kentucky farm, moved back "home," and enrolled at the nearby Frontier Nursing Service to study midwifery. Eventually Janice joined her. Mother and daughter shared a subscription to *Organic Gardening* and were "avid wild food foragers and gardeners together."

In the 1990s Janice found herself, somewhat reluctantly, in a local college finishing an elementary education degree. Recently divorced with two children, she needed to have an income. She explained, "I was a stay-at-home mom all those years, doing the gardening, cooking from scratch, making crafts, selling crafts." She continued, "I went to school, I tried to find a teaching position, was not successful, subbed for about five years. I finally decided I was going to do what I loved doing, which is being here, growing organic vegetables, and to see if I can sell them and make a living. The pivotal point was I got really sick last winter. I am tired of stressing out, worrying about getting a job, bending over backwards, trying to get a job." In many Kentucky counties, the school district is the largest and steadiest employer, and one with excellent benefits. Being hired in such a system can be highly political, as Janice learned.

In 2008, the summer following her illness, Janice became involved with World Wide Opportunities on Organic Farms (WWOOF). It is a clearinghouse for gardeners and farmers who need help and for people who want to travel and work while learning about sustainability and organic growing. In exchange, the farmer provides room and board. "I have always wanted to share my knowledge," Janice said, "so the WWOOF-ing is perfect. I need help to do what I want to do, because physically it's hard for me to keep up with it by myself. [The WWOOF-ers] value the things that I've grown up doing, and they want to learn, and that makes me feel validated. What I hope to work towards here is to create some educational workshops. I don't want to just grow to sell."

Not surprisingly, making money is never Janice's sole motivation. Her need to teach and share her philosophy is equal to her need to garden. She claims that she is not political, but her sense of how we should change our current agricultural system is quite radical. "If everyone tried to grow a little bit of their own food," she said, "no matter what, even if it is in a planter in a window or on a patio, it is just less of a carbon footprint. You're using less fossil fuel [than if you shipped] your food from California. I think people need to wake up and organize their priorities. Why do we need to get food from California? We can grow all the food we need here. It is amazing what some of the farmers are doing now. Just some of the small, little organic farmers [in Kentucky and Tennessee]."

Janice practices her philosophy. "I have always been passionate about trying to grow as much of my own food as I possibly can. I love everything. I like to grow every vegetable that it is possible to grow. So, in my garden, whether I am selling anything or not, I grow everything. I have always prided myself on being as self-sufficient as I possibly can. Along with that, goes to my commitment to make a difference in not destroying this planet. In growing my own food, I'm not supporting the shipping of food from all over the world to Kentucky. If I do buy something, say, we have a crop failure or we don't have fruit this year, I might buy a bushel of peaches to can, but they're from South Carolina. I buy as local as I can. I believe in living a simpler lifestyle that isn't destructive of the Earth and the resources we have."

An hour passed as we talked around Janice's kitchen table. We ate a beautiful and tasty vegetarian lunch including cornbread made with her homegrown and hand-ground Hickory King corn and a salad featuring chickweed and the flowers of wild violets that she foraged. I could sense, though, that Janice was ready to get back to the garden. In her own words, her work is "all consuming," but clearly she finds pleasure and satisfaction in it, too. "I love to grow my own food. It is such a fulfilling thing in my life to be out there doing everything it takes to grow my food and then working it up, canning it, freezing it, drying it, and eating it. It is such a healthy way to live. It is good exercise, it is fulfilling. It is awesome, healthy food."

ON A MISSION

Joe Trigg

JOE TRIGG HAS GARDENED all over the world——on a patio in Turkey, in a greenhouse in Las Vegas, and in discarded tires in England. When he was not gardening himself, he was observing agricultural practices in Israel, Bosnia, Egypt, Panama, and South Africa, all places he was stationed during his twenty-eight year air force career. As an explosive ordnance expert, he frequently served on the Secret Service's Very Important Personnel Protective Support Activity (VIPPSA), which accompanies heads of state and other dignitaries in conflict zones. But in 2007 Joe returned to his hometown of Glasgow, the county seat of Barren County, to teach others how to raise vegetables and provide healthy food to low-income people at affordable prices.

"I was born here," Joe told me. We were sitting in the walkout basement of his mother's nearly new home situated on the same expansive lot as the house in which Joe was raised. His boyhood household was headed by his mother and aunt and included Joe's four brothers, one sister, and two cousins, a boy and a girl. He continued, "Between my aunt and my mother we always had little gardens to help subsidize with food. You know when you grow up black and poor in rural America, you're doing everything you can." The Trigg family also raised chickens for eggs and meat. Joe had to weed and do anything else that his elders asked of him. His father's parents owned a farm in Metcalfe County. Joe and his siblings worked in their grandparents' garden, too, and helped in their and other farmers' fields with "hardcore crops" such as tobacco. "We were always taught that if you want something you got to work. You got to go to school, you got to get an education, and you got to work."

Joe looks like someone who has worked hard physically. He is tall, lean, and muscular. He acts like someone whose mind is spilling over with ideas and wants to share them. He speaks with a command of facts that he quickly stacks into a vision. Joe radiates physical and mental energy. I had to work to keep up with him. As co-owners of Trigg Enterprise, Joe, three of his brothers, and a cousin raise Black Angus cattle, grow vegetables to sell, and experiment with greenhouse culture.[43] As Joe puts it, "There's the beef part, the greenhouse part, and there's the field—sweet corn and watermelons and all that. We have a roadside stand [on the edge of my mother's yard], and then we have a mobile stand, which was originally set up for deliveries to the housing projects [in Glasgow and Louisville]." Joe is also a cofounder of Sustainable Glasgow, whose projects include starting Bounty of the Barrens Farmers' Market, where Joe is the only African American seller.

For those of us who are lucky enough to be able to shop at a local farmers' market, we likely have appreciative and friendly relationships with those from whom we buy but may not have an understanding of the political economy of the market and small-scale agriculture. Joe does. "When I was a kid, farmers' markets were where poor folks went to get their produce. [Studies now point out that they] are [mainly] financially feasible for the affluent [customer]." To have a viable system, Joe continued, "You have to have farmers [and] gardeners willing to grow the produce, you have to have some kind of distribution center, and then you have to have in place an indigenous market. The prices [at a farmers' market] are a little bit higher than [those at groceries and supermarkets,] and the original target group [that is, low-income people] of most farmers' markets is bypassed." Yet Joe acknowledged that farmer/gardeners who sell must make a decent profit. "Everybody knows raising a garden is hard work."

Joe and Trigg Enterprise intervened in this dilemma by creating Farmers 2 City Connection (F2CC). Like many of Joe's other efforts, this project, started in the summer of 2009, had several objectives. First, he wanted to train a new generation of black small farmer/gardeners. He targeted young African American landowners because the loss of black-owned land is, in his words, "staggering." He said that many of these farms have been out of production for some time and there is no working equipment. The "knowledge base has been lost for farming and gardening, in a lot of cases, but [there are those] willing to try to do something." Joe's goal was to help them "restore, maintain, and keep their potential asset"— the land. He wanted these new young farmers to use their land to "do good things" and to earn a decent living. *Doing good* in this case was taking locally grown fresh vegetables to residents in Louisville's low-income neighborhoods, the second objective of F2CC. Third, Joe wanted to see people's diets improve so they will be healthier. He wanted poor people to have an opportunity to eat high-quality, local, seasonal produce at prices they could afford. He hoped, at the same time, to educate people so they do not expect to have strawberries available year-round and will reject the tasteless "hard, green, gassed tomatoes in our grocery stores shipped in by agribusiness."

Farmers 2 City Connection had a rough first year. A grant application for needed equipment, especially a refrigerated truck to collect the produce in Glasgow for delivery to Louisville, was not funded. Joe had hoped to take in enough revenue to pay for the seed, transplants, plastic row cover, and equipment costs, much of which he had donated. It was "painful" for him when they did not do better that first growing season. He explained that he has retirement benefits from his military service but the livelihood of the others depended on the project. Joe said, "It was a negative start. But I'm an optimist. You got to start somewhere." Over the next few years, F2CC continued to falter. "Multiple factors led to [its demise]," Joe reasoned. "We started out with interest and participation from multiple farmers in multiple counties. Each year the numbers decreased and the amount of vegetables we had to grow went up." The demand increased, but Joe was unable to guarantee that the young farmers he was mentoring would come through. He moved to the community-supported agriculture, or CSA, subscription model to give "producers a more practical form of income." The young farmers' interest continued to dwindle. In 2013 the CSA was still intact, but Trigg Enterprise was the only producer and F2CC was closed.[44]

The optimism that sparked Farmers 2 City Connection was not without a foundation. Joe layers enterprise and sustainability into all phases of his undertakings. How vegetables are grown is as important to him as who is growing them and who has access to buy them. "What we're trying to do, gardenwise," he said, "is take old ideas that have been used all around the world [and implement them locally]. How can I make some of these processes feasible and then implement them here in the U.S. on a small scale?"

Joe has been toying with this question for years. While stationed at Nellis Air Force Base in Las Vegas in the 1980s, he experimented with an aquaponic system that used raised beds inside a small greenhouse. In aquaculture, or aquaponics, fish are raised in water and their waste is absorbed as fertilizer for plants; the plants, in turn, purify the water for the fish, in a circulating, self-sustaining system. A "raised bed" in this system refers not to one containing soil but to a box with a waterproof lining filled with water. Boxes are connected with piping that moves water from one bed to another. Sometimes they are arranged one after another on the ground, but the beds can also be stacked, bunk-bed style. Joe said, "I had an all-organic aquaculture." It was a "touchy system," an interdependent one, because if the fish die then the plants die and vice versa.

While stationed in Turkey, Joe had "three-hundred- to four- hundred-gallon fish tanks [filled] with hundreds of koi." He said, "I had vegetables out the yin/yang"; after providing for his own household, he gave the excess produce to other military families. In Panama, he observed more-traditional growing practices that also influenced his thinking. Joe said people

were still farming on a small scale, using the rotating system of their ancestors: burn the growth to clear the land, cultivate, allow the land to lie fal-
low, and repeat the process by burning off the regrowth. "We frown on
[these practices now]," he said. "As a country, we like farming with big tractors, big implements, twenty-five acres of tomatoes minimum, two hundred and fifty preferably, big chemicals, big pesticides, big everything."

The sustainable gardening methods that absorbed Joe during his military career continue to inform his practices today in Kentucky. He and his
brothers built a large greenhouse in his mother's two-acre yard in
Glasgow. Joe referred to this lot as the "research and test plot." For their
first project they planted eight hundred tomato plants from which they
hoped to harvest two thousand pounds of fruit a week. They had made
two deliveries when Winn Dixie, their contracted buyer, went bankrupt.
Undaunted, Trigg Enterprise began more diverse greenhouse culture
using hybridized processes: hydroponics mixed with bag culture with
"fertigation."[45] On my visit to the greenhouse, I saw bags—they look like
sawed-off gunnysacks or burlap bags, except they are made of a plasti-
cized woven material—filled with a soil medium sitting in orderly rows
on top of the ground. A tomato plant is growing out of each bag. It is
staked by an intricate system of overhead twine, wires, and tubing.[46] A
drip irrigation system provides water and nutrients. In another section of
the greenhouse were raised "beds" about four to five feet tall, full of
water. They looked like small bunkers. Laughing at his own zeal, Joe admitted that they had been "overbuilt, military style." But they were full of
small romaine lettuce plants, bobbing on top of the water in special trays.
They were being grown to sell to the Barren County school system, a
healthier and more local choice than the usual Californian-grown iceberg
lettuce served in the cafeterias.

Outside the greenhouse were multiple rows, over fifty feet long,
blanketed with white plastic. A drip irrigation system was hiding under
the covers. This area can be used to grow vegetables that need to
spread—melons or cucumbers, for instance. Joe talked in detail about

the most effective plastic to use in the rows and how the best irrigation drip tubing comes from Israel. He explained that white is the optimum color for the plastic "grow" bags and row covers because research has demonstrated that white decreases the number of bugs and pests, which, in turn, decreases the use of pesticides. In fact, Joe shuns chemical pesticides. He uses a host of gentle methods to fight the inevitable pests that can threaten crops—organic Safer's insecticidal soap, companion planting,[47] and aspects of integrated pest management (IPM).[48]

Joe is also an adherent of more traditional practices such as planting "by the signs" or "by the moon."[49] He and others who follow the "cycles" believe that the vitality and productivity of their vegetable crops are determined, in part, by the moon's revolution around the earth each month. Planting, weeding, and even pruning are determined by the phases of the moon. When Joe was a boy this information was usually accessed on a calendar distributed by the local insurance agent. Now websites exist that overlay moon cycles on the calendar with instructions on everything from when to plant which vegetable to when to weed.

Not a fan of big business or big agriculture, Joe rails against the influence these structures have in our society and how they thwart ecological and entrepreneurial interventions in garden and agricultural practices. "Big farming doesn't want anything that will make life easier for other folks," he said. "But folks in other countries look at the U.S. for innovation and ideas to help them do what they do—farming and gardening—better. And realize that they'll be able to do that without restriction." He provided an illustration. He has some plastic trays out in his greenhouse that were invented in the United States. They are designed to produce a better transplant and can be reused season after season. According to Joe, "big business" does not want those sold in the United States "because now you won't need to go to Walmart or K-Mart to buy your transplants, and you won't be buying new plastic cubes each year." Although the trays can be purchased in the United States, their cost is prohibitive if the object is to sell large quantities of cheap transplants, quickly. The irony, Joe said, is that Canadians, Europeans, and Mexicans use this particular system to produce the majority of their transplants, and it is the primary system for most tree nurseries in the world.

Joe takes these obstacles in stride. Even the skepticism of some of his neighbors and community cannot shake his optimism. "I think [we Kentuckians] can feed ourselves," he said, but "we can [only] feed ourselves seasonally." The greenhouse culture that he is constantly tinkering with is an effort to extend the growing season. He has grown vine-ripened tomatoes well into December. And he has grown cantaloupes and muskmelons—crops that require space and the right amount of rain in the dead of summer—vertically in the greenhouse, where he can better control temperature and moisture needs. "You have the naysayers," Joe said, "but when they drove by and saw [the melons], well . . ." His voice trailed off. I asked whether his neighbors think he is unusual. Joe said, "The proof is in the pudding."

I am convinced that Joe can do almost anything he sets out to do. I wondered, What drives him to innovate? Why is he so willing to experiment? Why does he see such possibility? I asked him these questions. His response surprised me, though in retrospect I see his logic. "The military," he answered. "A lot of things I did in the military was based on innovation. I won't go into the jobs I had, but you got to always be thinking and moving forward. We called it thinking outside of the box, 'cause you've got to be ahead of the next guy. You won't make it if you can't think out of the box." Joe was trained to scour an area for explosives to protect VIPs in war zones. His job was to see what others missed. The skills and mindset that guided him to think like the enemy and unearth danger are the same ones that drive him toward opportunity, action, and solutions. Where others perhaps see only intractable issues—the loss of black-owned land and black farmers, farmers' markets and healthy food affordable only by the affluent, a food supply primarily reliant on agribusiness, the lack of U.S. entrepreneurship in gardening and agriculture, and burgeoning health problems caused by poor diets—Joe sees health, restoration, and sustainable economies, systems, and lives. But he wants everyone to see the need for change and to understand that there is reason to be concerned. "The cocoon that you think you're living in isn't really a cocoon," he said.

After traveling all over the world and serving in multiple war zones, Joe Trigg is undoubtedly a reliable source on the nature of cocoons. And while many people might see Joe's coming back to Kentucky after a distinguished military career as a return to the cocoon, he knows differently. He sees the danger if Kentuckians—if Americans—do not transform our food supply and delivery system. That is why he is inventing and modifying the means for us to change, one experiment at a time.

THE LUCKY CROSS

Gary Millwood

GARDENING, COOKING, AND GIVING were constants in Gary Millwood's life.[50] He grew up at the end of the Great Depression in South
Carolina textile mill communities where his father, a "loom fixer," kept a
vegetable patch with cabbages, turnips, carrots, and tomatoes next to
their house. Though the family moved from one Spartanburg County mill
village to another—Valley Falls, Chesney, Beaumont—making a garden
was part of settling in at each new place. As Gary put it, "Everybody did
this." When he was a teenager, his mother, whose canned peaches "were a
work of art [that] looked like they had never been touched," also got a job
in the mill. She refilled bobbins. "That was when I developed my skills for
food. I would start something for dinner because she was at work," he
told me matter-of-factly, as if all boys cooked dinner for their mother. "As
a result of that, I developed culinary interests." And unlike his brothers,
who played league baseball all summer, Gary worked in the garden,
learning for a future he could not see then. He enjoyed it, "as long as [he]
felt helpful."

An ethos of giving, of being "helpful," became even more ingrained
when Gary followed his parents into the mill. Though a textile mill might
seem like an unlikely place for inspiration, Gary found it there. He explained that by the turn of the twentieth century the New England textile
industry had moved south looking for cheaper labor. They looked to the

mountains of North Carolina and South Carolina to recruit workers for their mills, promising housing and food. Some of Gary's North Carolina relatives on his father's side were persuaded. "What they didn't tell them," said Gary, "was about the company store [system]. It was a very paternalistic kind of community." He explained that it was not all bad, however: "[Working in the mill] was one of the best learning experiences I could ever have because it taught me that there was something better that I could put my life to. I decided I would go to school and work for the church. That's what I've been doing all my life."

After graduating from Presbyterian College in Clinton, South Carolina, and the Presbyterian School of Christian Education in Richmond, Virginia, Gary was prepared to teach and work with youth in the Presbyterian system of homes for children. Dotted throughout the South, these institutions historically served children who had been neglected, who had no parents, or whose family was unable to care for them. Gary said that the homes were meant to provide a place for these children to live and "to care for them and give them guidance."[51] From 1963 until he retired in 1999, Gary served variously as a teacher, food services manager, farm manager, and administrator at Presbyterian children's homes in Elon, North Carolina; Danville, Virginia; Brunswick, Georgia; and two separate stints in Louisville, Kentucky. At each of these posts, Gary brought together his culinary and gardening interests with his need to help.

At Louisville's Bellewood, where Gary spent the majority of his career, there was a farm and a garden to raise food for the residents as well as the staff, who usually lived on the grounds.[52] In the 1960s during Gary's first stretch at Bellewood, Fray Willhart, "a seasoned gardener," managed these enterprises, but when Gary returned in 1978 to finish his career, Fray had retired and Gary was responsible for everything—the children, the gardens, two hundred head of cattle, and all the pastureland. "I didn't have anybody to help me except the older kids," Gary said. "In that period of time, most of those children were long term. They had been there, they had worked for Fray." So with the children's help and that of his family—his wife and two sons—Gary managed. "It was an awful lot of pressure on me, [but] we finally were able to hire two people to take care of the cattle and maintenance." And with guidance from the Jefferson County Cooperative Extension, coupled with Gary's gardening background, Bellewood raised, among other things, corn, melons, beans, squash, pumpkins, tomatoes, lettuces, and cabbage. Following in Fray's footsteps, Gary and his helpers used manure from the cattle and leaves from the woodsy grounds to enrich the soil.

The culinary interests Gary developed as a young man took on new dimensions at Bellewood. Besides raising food, Gary oversaw the institutional kitchen where it was prepared. He remembered fondly two training sessions he attended at the luxurious Greenbrier Hotel in White Sulphur Springs, West Virginia, as "two of [his] best experiences." But he joked about "Sewageology University," the required Kentucky certification classes he attended on sewage treatment. Bellewood had its own wastewater treatment plant, and Gary was in charge of it, too.

Gary retired from Bellewood in 1999 not because he was ready but because his health had deteriorated seriously. He said, "I had angioplasty in the early nineties. Then in 1995 I had triple bypass surgery. [I] recovered beautifully, went back to work before the [recovery] time that was allotted." But in 1999 he had a second triple bypass operation and had to stop working. "I wasn't recovering," he said. "I couldn't get out of my chair. I was tired of watching TV. My wife continued to work, [but] I was sitting at home. When you stop working you feel like you're not productive anymore. So I developed all these slight depressions. I was feeling sorry for myself but then realized you got to do it yourself. So I decided what I'm going to do is start gardening some more. Doing it seriously." That's when Gary became a tomato head.

During his convalescence, Gary researched tomatoes. He chose heirloom tomatoes—particularly those that are rare and uncirculated. He began collecting seeds to grow plants in order to propagate, save, and distribute more seeds. He grew some of what he collected in containers, since bending down and digging in the ground became increasingly difficult for him. And he told me, "I have six foster tomato growers. I have tomato children." Together, they test and propagate seed, save the seed, and put it into circulation through enterprises such as Southern Exposure Seed Exchange, Baker Creek Heirloom Seed Company, and Seed Savers Exchange.

Gary also made a mark locally. For over a decade, each spring Gary took up residence at Louisville's Thieneman's Nursery to advise customers about growing heirloom tomatoes. He selected varieties for the greenhouse to grow and sell, and in exchange they let him propagate seedlings for his own use. At home where large blue containers, staggered, lined the side of his suburban house, he inspired and taught novice neighbor-gardeners. He said, "We live in a new subdivision. When we moved out there no one had gardens. But I have shared tomatoes with a bunch of people, and they are now growing for their children to experience." Gary

lived for these moments of social interaction, sharing, and spreading the word of the tomato. Gary's kindness and soft-spoken advocacy for the heirloom tomato were almost as irresistible as the names of the varieties he preserved. There are tomatoes named after people, such as Walter's Candy Stripe and Omar's Lebanese; those that refer to geography, such as Cowlick's Brandywine, Australian Heart, and Illinois Beauty; and those whose names describe their color, such as Amana Orange, Flamme Jaune, and Pink Boar. There is even a tomato (my favorite) whose name defies a stereotype: Royal Hillbilly. And one that depicts what everyone wants but is often elusive—Good Neighbor.

Some people take up bridge in retirement. I asked Gary, "Why tomatoes?" He began, "Because these were things that have lived in a period of time that people appreciated them. And they had some value to them." Gary, like many other passionate experts, then veered away from explaining the meaning of tomatoes toward sharing his catalog of knowledge. "I'm going to introduce you to a tomato today," he said, "the Aunt Lou, and you'll be the first one to taste it in Kentucky in about a hundred and fifty years because I found it in Ohio. Aunt Lou's Underground Railroad. We added the 'Underground Railroad' because it puts [the tomato] in historical perspective." The Aunt Lou seed was given to her by an African American man who escaped slavery in Kentucky by crossing the Ohio River to Ripley, Ohio.[53] I nudged Gary back to my original question. "I picked gardening," he said, "because it is part of nature, it is part of the cycle of things. You have the seasons—everything is changing from one to another. I felt like it would keep my interest the whole year long. When I'm not gardening, I'm sharing seed with people around the world. It rejuvenates your spirit to participate and be able to do these things. With the health problems I have—somebody called me the bionic man—I just sort of live day to day. I am experiencing each day as the gift of life, and gardening is helping me with that."

If Gary's life was on shaky ground, it did not stop him from experimenting with new techniques. As a pilot project, he planted an Aunt Lou and a Granny Cantrell tomato on each end of a bale of decomposing hay. The bale, like good soil, is both an anchor for the plant and the well from which the roots, leaves, and fruits draw nutrition. A bale of hay or straw is relatively mobile and can be placed on concrete or hardpan dirt where gardening would otherwise be difficult or impossible. "And they have been the two best-looking plants I've had this year," he declared. Maybe that is because the Aunt Lou tomato's survival is predicated on a slave's desire for freedom and the Granny Cantrell is the namesake of the first person to contribute to Gary's tomato seed bank. She died at age ninety-six, Gary said, and "she had grown that tomato all her life" in West Liberty, Kentucky. Freedom and fidelity are a powerful combination.

Gary knows this. Instead of retracting because of his health condition, Gary chose to expand and change to ensure the healthy continuation of Aunt Lou, Granny Cantrell, and all his other tomatoes. In 2009, he decided to replace unsustainable habits with organic methods, to "go purely organic," as Gary put it. Though in the past he had used Miracle-Gro on his tomatoes, he elected to shift to homemade compost tea. "I have lots of good recipes for it," he reported, and then launched one. "You take a five-gallon bucket and put a shovel full of good compost material into a bag that water can flow through—like a lingerie bag—[and put that in the bucket]. You put in a pump like you would use in a fish tank, and run it. In a day or two you add a variety of things. Molasses is one. If I am cooking something, I put in onion skins, husks from the corn, or [even] bad fruit [from] the refrigerator. I liquefy it in the food processor and add [the mixture] to the tea. After four or five days, it is ready. You dilute it: one gallon of tea to four gallons of water. Has to be rainwater or dechlorinated. You can use [it] as a foliar spray or drench [the plant]. This is a simple thing that people have been doing for a long time. They may not have used the aeration process. They may have stirred it. You can still do that. It just takes a little longer [to produce the tea]."

Gary was not really a stranger to organic growing; he had just gotten away from it. When he was a boy, he loved visiting his grandparents' farm in Spartanburg County and often spent several weeks in the summer there, learning and helping. "I didn't want to go home," he said. "It was more fun to be there than anywhere else." In those days, Gary remembered most gardeners and farmers as organic, using animal manures for fertilizer but having relatively few other interventions. One thing is for sure: it was at his grandparents' place that Gary began to appreciate the old-time varieties of fruits and vegetables, for one simple reason: the taste. He remembered that his grandfather had an apple tree. "I think implanted on my brain is the taste of that apple. I measure the taste of an apple by that apple I remember as a child." But not many today "measure up," he said decidedly.

Gary is probably right about that. I believe, though, that Gary measured up. As a young man, he aimed for "something better that [he] could put [his] life to." He always wanted to be helpful, and he was: by guiding and serving children living in the Presbyterian homes, by mentoring his tomato children, and by putting dozens of heirloom seeds in circulation. The outcome could have been quite different if Gary had not turned his capacity for caring toward himself. He designed a healing regimen—home gardening and home cooking combined with a save-the-tomatoes campaign. He made a new life for himself. If I had to pick a tomato name for Gary, I know what it would be. It is one heralded for its taste, texture, and reliability (the Brandywine) that mixed with an unknown yellow tomato to make a wonderful surprise of nature. The result is what many consider the best of the bicolored fruits. Undoubtedly, Gary is the Lucky Cross.

WASTE NOT, WANT NOT

Linda Rose

LINDA LITTLE ROSE was born in 1952 at the head of Big Spring Branch, near the mountain community of White Oak in Morgan County. Though in recent years some coal has been mined in nearby Magoffin County, nobody would consider Morgan County part of the eastern Kentucky coalfields. Instead it is known for an annual fall Sorghum Festival and the beautiful wide and fertile valleys formed by the Licking River. When a devastating tornado ripped through the largest town and county seat—West Liberty—in March 2012, Morgan Countians prayed at six funerals and then rolled their sleeves up to rebuild what was lost. Linda comes from people like this: people for whom faith and hard work are both means and end.

When Linda was four years old, her parents moved her and her older sister down the creek. They bought a farm that was close to the road and more accessible to the school bus. They left behind, but nearby, Linda's Little grandparents, as well as aunts, uncles, and cousins. Linda and her husband, Raymond Rose, raised their son in the farmhouse in which Linda spent much of her childhood; it is the same house where she lives today. Linda's sister still lives on Big Spring Branch, too, up the hill in the brick house their parents built in the mid-1960s.

These close and continuous ties to land, place, family, and community are reflected in the cadence of Linda's voice and in what she has to

say. Her concerns are about sustainability—environmental and cultural. Gardening is one of the primary ways that she understands and makes use of her past, but it is also the medium through which she does much of her work for change in hopes that we will have a future planet where gardens can thrive and environmental balance is restored.

As a young girl Linda remembers her grandfather Little plowing his garden and all the gardens along Big Spring Branch. "Papaw's mule," she reminisced. "When he would come plow there was no noise. Just the clink of the harness on the mule. He would sing religious songs in a beautiful deep voice. 'Never Grow Old.' 'Farther Along.' How sweet the soil [smelled]." But that impressionistic reverie of Linda's is complemented by practical wisdom. She said she comes from people who knew, "If you want to eat, you got to grow it. You have to sustain yourself in this world." Her mother's parents were "very, very poor. If they hadn't had a garden they'd probably have starved to death," Linda said. It is no wonder, then, that their daughter, Linda's mother, in addition to raising vegetables for her own family, created a gardening enterprise. She had a greenhouse and an acre of strawberries. She sold the berries and used the greenhouse to start vegetable plants for sale. While supplying local gardeners with what they expected, such as tomatoes and bell peppers, Linda's mother also introduced new tastes. "She was the first greenhouse around that had broccoli. Nobody knew what it was. She had a hard time selling it, because people would cut the flower off and try to eat the stem and the leaves. She had to educate people. She got the idea of broccoli from seed catalogs," Linda said." Mrs. Little also sold shucky beans and dried apples, and later, after Linda and her sister were grown, she made apple stack cakes for order.[54] She advertised her wares on the West Liberty radio station's live *Swap Shop* program, a form of free advertising in which sellers called in to the station to announce to listeners their merchandise for sale. As Linda said, "She was a real go-getter."

Linda and her sister were integral to their mother's enterprise. Their father, a construction foreman, worked long hours and, often, six days a week while Mrs. Little oversaw the life of the household and the farm. The two girls and their mother worked hard. "If she had any [extra] time, she'd sit down and crochet," Linda said. "She thought idle hands was the devil's workshop. She didn't believe in taking a nap through the day. That was a waste of life." But there was not that much extra time, especially during the growing season. If they were not planting, cultivating, or harvesting, then they were preparing food for canning, freezing, or drying. Linda explained, without rancor, "We'd break beans for days on the porch until your fingers would be pushed back from your nails and they'd be so sore. We'd peel apples even if we only got one little good piece from it." Because the Littles did not spray their fruit trees, in some years the apples would be so wormy there was not much left to save. And if Linda was not assisting with food preservation she was observing it, such as when her Little grandparents made "shuck sausage." Linda described the process:

"After they killed a hog, they made their sausage and rolled it up. They got a nice clean [corn] shuck; they would drop [the sausage] in there and then pull the shuck up over [the sausage], tie it, and let it age [in the smokehouse]." Linda paused, then added this modern update for those who do not have a smokehouse, "Today you can let it age in your refrigerator for a while to get that shuck taste."

It is obvious that Linda was taught to make the most of everything they grew, from canning or drying every last green bean to using even the smallest good part of a wormy apple to transforming leftover corn shucks into flavorful sausage casings. Naturally, they saved seeds—sometimes for longer than one might suspect. Linda remembered a dipper gourd that her grandfather had grown. Her mother wondered whether the seeds inside it would grow even though it was at least twenty years old. Linda said, "We cut a little hole in it, got some seeds, and they grew." This sensibility infused all household operations. "We didn't even have a garbage can, because we didn't even have any garbage or trash," Linda explained. "There was no waste. We used every little piece. I couldn't even get material to make doll clothes, because if it was an inch by inch [remnant], Mommy would put it in a quilt. There was no throwaway."

Today, Linda still strives to produce no waste. "Recycle, reduce, and reuse" is her mantra. But she remains open to fresh ideas and does not let the past rule her. Informed by reading magazines such as *Organic Gardening* and *Mother Earth News,* Linda has become an organic gardener. She believes that "if a [gardening] method hurts something there should be a better way to do it." She used to grow her vegetables in long rows with dirt between each row, as her parents had always done. The weeds that thrive in the space between the rows had to be hoed or tilled frequently so that they did not get the best of the garden. "But then I figured out it was so much better to section it off [with paths of grass in between planting areas]," Linda said. "I'd rather mow as hoe. And also [the grass paths] help hold your moisture in and the earthworms have a little place to stay and you have a nice place to walk." Linda's parents, as did many home

gardeners of the time, used DDT in the 1950s and 1960s to ward off pests such as potato and bean beetles. They switched to Sevin when DDT was outlawed in 1972 by the Environmental Protection Agency. But Linda said that garden pests have become immune to the string of pesticides introduced by chemical companies and that the "environment is out of balance." To control the destructive bugs in her garden she uses a variety of methods. "I try to pick off all the bugs I can, and if it gets beyond, we only use organic [pesticides]. I try crop rotation, and I do try to pick varieties [of vegetables depending on their local disease resistance]." She added, "I don't believe in the GMO [genetically modified organism] seeds. It kills the bees; it kills the microorganisms in the soil."

Considering Linda's upbringing, one that combined extensive home food production with a mandate to conserve and recycle, it is not surprising that she landed a job as the PRIDE (Personal Responsibility in a Desirable Environment) coordinator in Morgan County. She works with the public schools to teach children about gardening, environmental health, and energy conservation.[55] "Children can find just everything they need in our environment," she said. "And gardening is seventy-five percent of that." She works hard to find effective and interesting ways to bring children into the garden while also undermining their prevailing logic about "pests." She said, "I think of bumblebees as precious. So many of the kids want to kill everything that comes in their sight." But when they start swatting, she tells them, "Don't do it. You don't go to the zoo and kill the animals, [so] don't go to your outdoor classroom and kill what's out there."

Linda hopes to capture as many children as she can in the web of gardening. She wants to transform them into what she calls "a picky bunch." This is how she refers to her own family and their need to grow and eat their favorite variety of each vegetable. She said, "Once you start [gardening], it is in you. You have to [do it]. You feel this melancholy feeling [if you don't have the vegetables you like]. When I want a yellow Yukon potato I go dig it. That's what I want. You can't always find that at

the store. My strawberries, my raspberries, my rhubarb—I want my own. I grow certain kinds of beans, old-fashioned heirlooms. And Marconi peppers. I want mine. I don't remember ever seeing them in the store." She and her husband, Raymond, even raise a specific variety of corn called Boone County White for meal that they have ground at William Walter's mill in Morgan County. "I don't like brought-on.[56] It doesn't have a good taste." And perhaps to explain her discernment in matters of cornmeal, she added, "I was raised on cornbread."

Though Linda's personal history has shaped her proclivities—recycling, gardening, conservation—she is living solidly in the twenty-first century. People's relationship to the past is rarely static. Her grandparents, for instance, did not grow Yukon Gold potatoes or Marconi peppers, but they did teach her how to make shuck sausage. And while Linda's parents grew Boone County White, a corn developed in the nineteenth century, for the meal in their daily cornbread, they also embraced the wonders of DDT. Today Linda grows a garden as if her life depended on it but without using chemical pesticides. Sustainability is not about living in the past, nor is it about being fearful of the new. But it is about rethinking and undoing our current patterns of throwaway hyperconsumption. What food we eat, how we obtain it, who grows it, and how they grow it are key questions we must pose about a sustainable future. Linda asks these questions. And she teaches her students to do the same.

One of the many beautiful qualities in Linda is her ability to see small, everyday possibilities embedded in larger concerns. For example, while talking about the plentiful, local black walnut and hickory trees, she said, "People don't take advantage of what's dropping off in their [own] yards." If people would only pick up the fallen nuts and work the nutmeats out, they would have delicacies for baking and for simply eating, she explained. "The walnuts are full of everything people need [nutritionally]. And you can't buy that at Walmart."

The other thing you cannot buy is someone like Linda who means what she says and says what she means. She put the "grit" in "integrity." "I'm particular," she said. "Nobody can satisfy me. Satisfy yourself. I don't look to the world to satisfy me." But she does want the world to take stock of our current ecological calamity. Maybe if we could build a society that engenders and prizes personal integrity undergirded by an ethos of sustainability—Linda's domain—we might save ourselves while being ourselves.

LEAFY GREENS ARE WHERE IT'S AT

Dave Kennedy

DAVE KENNEDY is a people's scientist with a flair for low-tech, sustainable solutions. His laboratories are gardens around the world. The results of his experiments show that the answer for malnourishment is located not in bigger, better farms and engineered food but in local gardens growing indigenous plants. As he told me, "I think there are some heroic farmers out there, but ultimately what we need is fifty million gardeners."

A gentle giant, Dave is well over six feet tall, with broad shoulders and big hands that look accustomed to manual labor. I could picture him turning the long rows of compost that lined the road we walked on from my car to his house. He moves surprisingly gracefully, almost like a dancer.

After meeting Dave, I could not help but see him as a product of two powerful, mythical themes in the post–World War II American consciousness: the homogeneity of suburbia and the nonconformity embodied by hippies. How we treat our land and what it means to us—central features of these dueling stories—are guiding questions for Dave. His story of living on the land, of going back to the land, is illustrative of our long-held tension between a professed love of owning part of the Earth while simultaneously treating it with disrespect. This national contradiction has been the terrain upon which his life's work has unfolded.

Dave's parents were descendants of those forced to leave Ireland and migrate to North America during the nineteenth-century potato famine. They sought out the sprouting suburbs on the edges of metropolitan areas in the years following World War II. One of the ironies of the new suburban ethos was that one could own land but not be bound by it. A livelihood was derived elsewhere. The yards in many of these suburbs were often as indistinguishable from one another as the houses (and that remains true today). These new geographical and spatial forms afforded an alternative kind of privacy and demarcation between neighbors. Yards were decorative units of separation. They were to be manicured by using an arsenal of yard tools and, eventually, chemicals. Suburban yards, as initially lived in, were most decidedly *not* meant to contain vegetable or herb gardens or fruit trees. This is the world in which Dave, born in 1947, was raised.

Dave's father was a traveling salesman, a job that caused his family to move "every couple of years" to places in Michigan, New York, Massachusetts, and Pennsylvania. On the road he sold Junket and My T Fine pudding mixes. When he came home, he was "domineering." Dave's mother, "overwhelmed" and "shut down," was a housewife, raising a daughter and three sons. Dave described his growing up as "a kind of shapeless cultural upbringing." His relationship to land was defined by mowing the lawn. He told me that he "didn't know how to do anything." He said, "I was really a fully dysfunctional person. I'd spent twelve years in school almost completely nodded out. I'd set my awareness to a level that I wouldn't get in big trouble. It was really wasted time." When he entered Bucknell University in Pennsylvania, he did not last long.

What did a middle-class kid from suburbia do in 1966 when he flunked out of college? "I became a hippie. I lived on the streets in Washington, [DC;] then I moved to Boston. I lived in Cambridge." Cambridge in 1967 and 1968 was "like a hundred thousand street freaks and their free music and camps in the parks." Dave made his living doing odd jobs: "I'd work as a janitor, Handy Andy, sell blood, [do] psychological experiments at

Harvard . . . for ten dollars a test." By the early 1970s, however, "the city started to get ugly. There was a lot of heroin coming in. It just seemed like it had played out. The flower-child thing was running out of steam. There were more hard drugs [and] hard politics. The love part was slipping to the background."[57]

The military had rejected Dave because it found him to "respond marginally in structured situations," so for him, the Vietnam War was not the personal specter it was for so many other draft-age young men. Once again, rejecting the trappings of a conventional life, Dave moved to the New Hampshire woods with his girlfriend, Mimi. He bought half an acre inside a seven-square-mile tract for fifty dollars down and twenty dollars a month. They arrived with an eighteen-dollar used army tent in a "'61 Plymouth Belvedere [traded] for four ounces of pot from Big Ed Fish. We were in this place where we thought, 'We live in the country and we'll grow our own food and we won't have to have a job.' Seven square miles of woods is a lot of freedom." There, in the shade of a pine forest, Dave planted his first garden. "We were so stupid," he remembered. Borrowing a phrase from Stephen Gaskin of the commune known as The Farm, Dave remembers these early experiences as occurring in the "home for the criminally naïve."[58]

What the military should have realized about Dave is that he responds doggedly to marginal situations. He knew nothing about construction but built a cabin from recycled materials, including stolen road signs—all for thirty-two dollars. Yet even with the new house, he remembers "waking up one morning [to find it] zero inside." In due time, Dave joined the Northeast Organic Farming Association (NOFA), through which he and Mimi met a local farmer who offered them a "funky" house to live in and some land for raising a garden, in exchange for labor. "Rural New Hampshire was being depopulated. The farms were all folding. It was a hard place to make it as a farmer. And new people were coming in. And the old people didn't have any respect for the young people, but on another level they had some sense that 'this is good, somebody is coming in here trying to pick up the baton even if they're complete idiots and they look like freaks.'" Eventually, the farmer agreed, in exchange for half of their profit, to let Dave and Mimi use three and a half acres and his equipment to grow vegetables organically. NOFA would then sell and distribute the produce. Customers included black community activists operating feeding programs in New York City, illustrating the remaining political connections between urban leftists and radical back-to-the-land hippies. But distribution proved to be an insurmountable obstacle because their dilapidated vehicles were not reliable.

Still, these experiences in New Hampshire provided Dave with new skills and the time to formulate a philosophy, both of which set him on the course on which he remains today. "I was very romantic about nature," he explained. "I would climb these white pine trees until the very top where they're real flexible and just blow in the wind." From his perch he could hear approaching chainsaws and bulldozers mowing down trees to make way for a new road. Dave reasoned that humans, his species, are "trashing nature to build this road, and as soon as they build that road they're going to put crap along it." He recalled, "I thought, 'I've got to do something about this.'" He spent about three days in his lean-to in the woods wondering what to do. "I had this thought to learn everything I could about food because food was this place where the human world and the natural world came together. Everybody had to eat it: rich, poor, black, white, men, women. Everybody eats food. That really spun me off in a different direction."

Even though Dave had never finished college, he entered a master's program at Goddard College to study food systems. With low-residency requirements, Goddard, located in Vermont, was interested in people who wanted to research a topic and use it for social action. These radical pedagogical guidelines suited Dave, and he completed his degree.

In the mid-1970s, a hard freeze one New Hampshire August that killed the tomatoes and other crops made Dave and Mimi head south, looking for a more temperate climate. They landed in a community called

Door Ajar that collectively owned eighty acres near Alexandria, Tennessee. Located in DeKalb County, it was "out in the middle of nowhere [with] no electricity," as Dave described it. He explained that the group was into "obsessive gardening"; because they had no money, they were gardening to eat. They made compost, cleared land, and dug ponds. "We just did a lot of stuff by trial and error. Made a lot of errors." Mimi eventually left for New Mexico, while Dave continued to persevere and thrive in what most would consider marginal circumstances even as Door Ajar morphed into Flat Rock Community. But after more than fifteen years in existence the community "was starting to unravel. There was a lot of political strife," and as Dave explained, "people were developing different interests." In 1991 Dave moved to Lexington in order to stay close to his young son, Rafael, whose mother had begun attending graduate school at the University of Kentucky.

Dave is a man who laughs at himself easily and freely. When I commented that he had stayed in the back-to-the-land collective longer than most, he quipped, "Like I said, I am a slow learner. I stayed in it longer, then started it again here." During the Lexington period, Dave did backyard gardening. Eventually, he and his partner separated, and he grew restless to live again in the country. He cofounded the community of Egret's Cove, outside of Berea, Kentucky, near the junction where Madison, Rockcastle, and Jackson Counties meet. "I have this political/philosophical bent towards what I would describe as an Arcadian view," he told me. "There is the city of man and the wilderness of nature, and then there's this theoretical place—Arcadia—where the two come into harmonious [balance]." For Dave, "nature" is the garden and the "city of man" is the enlightened village. His project is to create a "rural renaissance around the formation of little villages or pods where you have interesting conversations." For example, he said, "In our community in Tennessee we'd have these study groups, and every week someone would lead one. So you might have one on urban-rural contradictions or the role of women or early childhood education. It was kind of like a rich mental life in a rural area where typically the idea [is] that you got to leave the rural area to go to the city to have a richer cultural and mental life. We [were] trying to work around that." To complement these intellectual pursuits, Dave and his collectives have been trying to tread lightly on the Earth by building modest-size houses from recycled and salvaged materials and developing edible green manures. Dave, in other words, has been pursuing sustainability since long before it became mainstream, ever since he was sitting in the tops of the swaying pine trees in New Hampshire at the beginning of the 1970s.

Dave defies powerful, stereotypical images of the reclusive back-to-the-lander and the hedonistic hippie. One of his most passionate goals is to transform leafy greens into a global antidote for malnourishment and a strategy for sustainability. Good for body and soil, edible green manures allow the grower to amend the soil while keeping the ground in production for food. Leafy greens, with their rich store of nutrients, can be used for food first, then worked back into the dirt to improve its texture and increase its fertility. These green cover crops also eliminate the need for chemical fertilizers that ultimately deplete the soil while also requiring fossil fuels to produce. And leafy green manures are better than animal manure because most animals have been fed grains that, in general, are produced by using petrochemicals (such as fertilizer and diesel fuel for the tractors). Green manures are sustainable. "You can grow [leafy greens] as green manures, take some percentage of that crop as a leaf crop, dry it, and add twenty percent of that dried leaf crop into [food]. You get all kinds of vitamins and protein from it," Dave explained.

Although I think of myself as a well-informed gardener who has used cover crops to improve the clay soil I have often encountered in my Kentucky gardens, Dave's leafy greens strategy was new to me. While I have considered my garden a source of food and pleasure for family and friends, Dave has been asking for years: What is the smallest space on which all the nutrients necessary for a family of four could be

grown? In his research, Dave found that leaf crops will produce more nutrients per square foot than other foods. As Dave explains, the protein is in the leaf, so if you separate out the fiber (the stems, for example), a highly concentrated source of nutrition remains. In the early 1980s, Dave joined with Find Your Feet, an organization in England that made a leaf concentrate from alfalfa and mustard greens, among other plants, that was 55 percent protein.[59] Find Your Feet asked him to go to Mexico, and eventually other countries, to work on projects with rural people to eradicate malnourishment through leafy greens.[60] Dave founded Leaf for Life in the United States and wrote a manual on leaf extracts. He has been recognized by the United Nation's Food and Agriculture Organization (FAO) as an expert on the subject; in 2009, he was invited to a symposium in Paris hosted by the Association pour la Promotion des Extraits Foliaires en Nutrition (Association for the Promotion of Leaf Extracts in Nutrition). In 2010 the FAO published the book *Combating Micronutrient Deficiency: Food-Based Approaches,* to which Dave contributed a chapter cowritten with leaf concentrate researchers in England and France.[61]

Always tinkering with ideas to improve everyday lives, Dave designed solar dryers for dehydrating greens—a much simpler and less energy-intensive process than leaf extraction. Dave said, "We'll go into a town in, say, rural El Salvador and talk to people, and the next day we can make solar dryers with the women, and the next day after that, the kids in the school will be eating cookies made with the [solar-dried leafy greens]." One of the reasons nutrition is compromised in these areas is because of agribusiness. Many Americans might assume, for example,

Butterfly pea, *Clitoria ternatea,* a native of southeast Asia. Dave Kennedy is interested in this plant because "it is an excellent source for making leaf concentrate and a good nitrogen fixer."

that in rural Brazil, farmers are growing and eating beans, their own locally produced protein. But Dave is seeing how corporate agricultural enterprises have changed local patterns. Instead of growing the beans they have historically cultivated, small farmers have replaced them in recent years with the more lucrative soybean, sold as a cash crop to agricultural conglomerates. The health of the community declines in this exchange. Paradoxically, this situation is what makes the leafy-greens interventions successful. Dave explains, "One of the nice things about leaf crops, there's not a big international market for it. They don't have any shelf life. They're almost inherently a local crop. They don't lend themselves to being taken over by Monsanto."

From Dave's view, Monsanto and their ilk are examples of a larger problem. "Farming is obnoxious," Dave asserted. "Farming is played out. Farming has this mathematical/mechanical model to where it is all growing for money, it is all on too big of a scale. They can't take care of the land. They're way tied into machinery. Everything is essentially taking that Henry Ford assembly line [model] and trying to slap it over a biological reality. It is just brutal." He goes on, "The farming thing is kind of done anyway. There are more people in prison than there are farmers in the United States. We have lost our way. We've really lost our relationship with nature. That, to me, is like the heart of what is good about gardening. It is a way back into the natural world. The kids here, [in Egret's Cove,] they take out the garbage and pour it in [the compost bin], and then in the spring there's a compost pile. Now there's a new cabbage that we grew with the peels from the old cabbage. Cycles. It is not just a new cabbage because we drove to Kroger's again and got this shrink-wrapped thing." Laughing at himself, Dave stops. "I'm ranting."

If Dave is ranting, I am not offended. We can be blinded by what we see as commonplace. But a bird's-eye view can reveal a reality that is different from the perspective on the ground. Dave experienced this from his perch atop the New England white pines. And what the army determined was Dave's failing—an inability to flourish in "structured situations"—gave, and continues to give him, the freedom to create an alternative vision. The first step of that vision is understanding that agribusiness contributes to the malnourishment of body and land. Practicing the leafy green remedy—one that is local, organic, and sustainable—is the second. And until we truly realize that our own health depends on caring for the health of the Earth, ranting might be a necessary third.

INSIDE OUT

Seema Capoor and Ashish Patel

GARDENING IS an all-out sensory experience for Seema Capoor and Ashish Patel. They are as interested in the aesthetics of their plantings as they are in the smells and tastes that come from their herbs, vegetables, and flowers. The world they have built outside their house is a reflection of the life they have made inside, where fragrant, delicious, and gorgeous food is crafted. Overarching both is a less-is-more philosophy combined with an environmental consciousness. Their passive solar home stays comfortable, without air conditioning, even on the muggiest Kentucky summer day. Constructed of native stone and wood, the house sits on top of a hill in Madison County on a finger of land formed by a U-curve in the Kentucky River. It stands out architecturally from the other, more conventional, homes in the rural subdivision, but the nonlawn surrounding the house makes a mark, too.

Instead of hauling in truckloads of topsoil and sod and then spreading fertilizers and herbicides to make a massive weed-free lawn on the thin rocky soil, Seema and Ashish opted for a more natural, organic approach. They discovered that if left alone the yard would exhibit a seasonally shifting variety of blooming native plants that Ashish called "wonderful gems" and that other people, Seema said, probably think of as "weeds." When Ashish's parents come for a visit from India, they ask, "How come your lawn is so poor and everyone else's is so perfect?" Ashish said that a lawn is "essentially phoniness. What looks good is actually a bed of chemicals and poisons, and the runoff is messing up the river which is right here. The whole story about the perfect lawn [is that] billions of dollars are spent a year in this country just to have something that looks good but that deep inside is actually a huge problem. And bees, butterflies, insects are all disappearing because of this." In contrast, their meadow-like "lawn" is humming with native pollinators—bumblebees, sweat bees, mason bees. And they have added a honeybee hive, carefully selected native plants, and built raised beds, formed by dry-laid Kentucky fieldstone walls, spilling over with a mixture of herbs, vegetables, and flowers.

Living in Kentucky may have given Seema and Ashish their first opportunity to grow a vegetable garden, but their love of plants began in their hometown of Bombay, India, as they were growing up in the late 1960s and '70s.[62] As a young boy Ashish lived in a densely populated suburb, where everyone lived in apartment buildings. His building had about a three-foot-wide perimeter "where a few random trees were growing. There was no focus on landscaping," he said. But often those trees provided a seasonal fruit or flavoring for a home-cooked dish. Ashish remembered the indigenous mulberries and *jamun,* "fruits which were plucked from trees but nobody intentionally planted them." And there was a tree whose hanging pods looked like drumsticks. Each pod of the native *Moringa oleifera,* or drumstick tree, "is a long bean with a sticky inside which is used in cooking, especially in lentil curries. Once a year some guy would scale the tree and get all [the pods] down and distribute them among the families. For that one week we would eat that." When Ashish was around ten years old, his family built a house, designed by his uncle who was an architect. Closer to the sea than his old neighborhood, the new home sat on small parcel of drained land that had once been a swamp. "That's where the gardening took off," Ashish said. Both his parents are medical doctors, but his father had retained an interest in gardening since boyhood. He had come from a farming background in rural Gujarat, a state north of Bombay. He tended outside potted plants, and as Ashish described, "There was a lawn with Bermuda grass, and for privacy screening, it was different colored bougainvillea, and some nice tropical vines with very fragrant flowers. [But] never vegetables. There was never any food grown at our house except for an attempt at celery. And we did have a lime tree."

Seema grew up in Bombay and in London, England. In Bombay, she lived in apartments; because her mother worked as a schoolteacher and her father as a commercial airline pilot who was often away from home, there was "no time or room for plants," Seema said. But she "marveled" at neighbors who did tend houseplants on their balconies. During her teenage years, her father was posted in London, where they had a house, and she watched him tend cucumbers and tomatoes in the backyard. Seema said that to grow vegetables was "in his genes," because even though he grew up in the city of Allahabad, his family lived in a house with a plot of land where they grew mostly fruit but some vegetables and kept a milk cow as well.[63] Seema's initial flirtation with hands-on plant care began, she said, when "a friend presented [her] with a magnolia sapling. Then came a few houseplants here and there, and it just took off." After she entered medical school in London she continued her love affair with potted plants: they brought her pleasure, and they could be cared for inside when no outdoor space was possible.

Seema had yet another way of satisfying her senses with botanical beauty that did not require actual land to cultivate. When she and Ashish, who is also a physician, moved to Philadelphia to begin the long certification process for practicing medicine in the United States,[64] she steered them to the formal, parklike Longwood Gardens and the spectacular Philadelphia Flower Show. By the summer of 1995, Ashish had completed his U.S. medical training, and he then entered a private internal medicine practice in Manchester, a small mountain town in eastern Kentucky. He and Seema rented a house in nearby London, where at last they had land and the requisite hot summers for raising vegetables. And, best of all, they had an eighty-year-old neighbor named Archie who was a seasoned gardener and a gifted mentor. "I think what we were doing at that time was trying to grow things that we couldn't easily buy," Seema said. For the food they liked to cook, they needed, among other things, okra, fenugreek, basil, chili peppers, and ichiban eggplant,[65] all of which were then hard to find in their local supermarkets. So that is exactly what they planted in their first Kentucky vegetable garden.

When they moved the fifty miles north from London to Richmond, Seema and Ashish left a garden and Archie for a duplex with a balcony. But the change meant that Seema, who is an ophthalmologist, could have a reasonable commute to the University of Kentucky, where she had landed a position as a researcher that would eventually lead to her acceptance into the residency program. Ashish moved his practice to Richmond in Madison County. They learned how to grow chili peppers and basil in pots that shared the deck with the orchids and gardenias that Seema had carted from Philadelphia to Kentucky. Seema recalled, "There wasn't much place for us to sit [outside in the summer]."

Moving to a home without a proper garden was not the letdown it could have been. Many of Ashish's patients, as it turned out, were gardeners from the surrounding countryside. Ashish, who has never met a stranger and is interested in agriculture, animal husbandry, apiculture, and gardening, is as capable of conversing as he is at diagnosing. His patients must agree, because in the gardening months they ply him with tomatoes, turnips, and beets. Sometimes a patient shows up with a crate of green beans to share with the doctors, staff, and even other patients. Ashish said, "I have this [patient] who brings me—neatly labeled and cleaned—eight or nine kinds of vegetables in ziplock bags. It isn't for the freezer [but] is just the way she presents it. It is beautiful."

After Seema and Ashish moved into their new ridgetop home in the summer of 2003, they were no longer confined to gardening on a deck. But even with all the land they now have, Seema said, "We haven't felt the need to grow so many vegetables because we are given so much." Ashish, who can have a devilish sense of humor, continued, "Why would

I grow tomatoes when these guys are bringing me eight or nine different varieties, from yellow to cherry? Then I get the word out that I really like okra, and lo and behold next year someone brings me two bags of okra." But Ashish also asks his patients for gardening advice. Beets were a case in point. A patient advised Ashish how to raise beets. The next spring this patient brought Ashish "grapefruit-size" beets, but Ashish, who had faithfully followed his patient's instructions, produced beautiful green tops with "marble-size beets." "We planted at the same time," Ashish lamented. "So the skill is definitely lacking here. I am farming challenged." "Not for lack of trying," Seema said.

Given the bounty that Ashish's patients supply, Seema and Ashish can concentrate on herbs and vegetables that are particular to their native cuisine and can still be hard to find locally in optimum condition: curry plant, thyme, basil, cilantro, lemongrass, oregano, mint, ginger, okra, and eggplant. They also grow purslane and arugula for their salads and edible flowers such as nasturtiums to embellish a platter of food. They have experimented with cultivating soybeans, and Seema hopes that her pomegranate and guava trees will one day bear tasty fruit. Shunning chemical fertilizers, they have learned about the beneficial practice of rotating crops and worked to improve the tilth and fertility of their soil by additions of organic matter. Rain barrels catch roof water to use for plant watering, and a cistern to increase their collecting capacity is under consideration. As Seema said, "[We] stick with what is natural."

Seema, however, is not a purist. She loves native plants as much as Ashish does but cannot help herself when it comes to exotic plants.[66] Ashish said, "I am dismayed by the stacks of these [plant] catalogs that keep coming. And there is a constant battle. The minute I get it, I try to toss it or hide it, and somehow, like a dog sniffing out moles, Seema finds these catalogs." She educates herself with the catalogs and orders from them, too. In the winter, their home is filled with potted plants—jasmine, gardenia, plumeria, an olive tree seedling, a cutting of this and that from the person who is in charge of a greenhouse near her hospital and whom

Seema has charmed. In the summer, all the plants are moved outside, blocking walkways and taking up much of the seating area. When she comes home from work, she will go "around and look at every plant," Seema said. Ashish likens this habit to that of doctors making their rounds. "We go and check each patient," he said. "When she comes home, it is these rounds: examination, diagnosis, and the joy of seeing this new flower or something that has survived from last year." Part of Seema's project, she said, is "evok[ing] the surroundings in which [they] grew up." In the summer especially, because they do not use air conditioning, they have what Ashish called a "blind man's garden" like in India when many of the most perfumed flowers open at night and fill the house with "sweet fragrances."

The design of their home and garden and the way in which Seema, Ashish, and their two daughters, Ananya and Avanti, choose to inhabit it blur the boundaries between indoors and outdoors—as much as one can in Kentucky, where four distinct seasons affect our growing and social practices. "The house was designed with that in mind, trying to connect the inside with the outside," Seema explained. But as Ashish described, they, too, are part of this deconstruction of the long-held "truth" that nature exists outside and people, who are ostensibly separate from nature, live inside. "What I've realized with this house is our connection to the environment, the weather, the seasons," Ashish said. "Because our plants are so affected by these things and because it is such an open house, we know when there is a full moon. We know when there is a clear sky that there will be a frost here. And that has enhanced our awareness of nature and who we are in our surroundings."

Seema and Ashish built a house that "is a little different" and made a garden that "is a little different," as they put it. What maybe they did not bargain for was how much their ties to nature would deepen by living in a place that attempts to turn outside/inside inside out. We cannot all build houses and gardens like theirs, but we can turn Ashish's phrase into a question and ask ourselves, "Who are we in our surroundings?"

OF ONIONS AND TIME

Gloria and Don Williams

EVEN THOUGH I have lived in Kentucky for over forty years, I had never been to Menifee County until I visited Gloria and Don Williams one warm May morning at their ridgetop farm. We sat on their front porch to do the interview even though one of their biddy hens, sitting on her eggs nearby, kept fussing at us. The birds were chirping so vociferously that their song is now immortalized on my tape recording. A constant breeze came across the hills, keeping us comfortable, even as the day heated up. All of us were feeling, I think, a little shy. But I was grateful that I had finally come to this scenic county of small farms and homeplaces that dot the hilly countryside, creating a foil for the rugged and spectacular Red River Gorge just beyond.

It would be hard to imagine people and a place more bound together than Gloria, Don, and Menifee County. Gloria was born in 1947 and has always lived on these 101 acres that are about seven miles from the county seat of Frenchburg. Her father, Jake Powers, was raised on this land. Gloria's mother, Geneva, was also born in Menifee County. She still lives in the family home about a hundred yards away from Don and Gloria's house. Don's mother, Golden, was from Menifee County. Don, who was born during the Great Depression in 1934, grew up on forty acres near the community of Pomeroyton, about ten miles from where he and Gloria live. Don and Gloria are the keepers of this place and of the traditional practices that have given the land life and breath all these years. The land has been good to them, and they are good to it.

Don drew a picture of his early life as one steeped in horticultural and agricultural knowledge and one in which being a good neighbor was both necessary and cherished. He said, "We lived off the farm one hundred percent except maybe for some coffee or sugar. Potatoes, corn, beans, and tomatoes—that was the four main crops that we growed, to put vegetables in the cellar [and] to eat. With Dad, we had a big orchard. We had plenty of apples. He had a grape arbor. We had plenty of grapes. We made juice and grape jelly. But, see, with eight kids plus the parents, it took a lot to eat. Mommy would can four to five hundred jars of vegetables every year. Dad grew his hogs, three or four big hogs every year. We had chickens all the time. My dad grew cane to make molasses out of. We had a good life. It was a life that neighbors visited neighbors. People was close. If one family got down and out, the other families would come in to help. We growed up conservative, but we didn't go hungry." Don remembers them as "happy days." He continued to contribute to his family well into adulthood. "Then after I got up and gone," he told me, "I helped support my family for years and years and years, even after I got married."

By contrast, Gloria was an only child. "I was always the boy my dad never had. I wasn't an inside person, and I'm still not. So I was always out farming and cattle wrestling with my Dad," Gloria said. The Powers family raised tobacco as well as a hardy garden. Like Don's mother, Geneva Powers also canned and preserved food from what they raised. A skilled carpenter, Mr. Powers built the house that Gloria grew up in, as well as the house where she and Don now live. "I can drive through the county and see lots of houses my dad built," Gloria observed proudly.

Don and Gloria's marriage is as solid as their knowledge about gardening. When I asked how they met, Don, looking a bit sheepish, took control of the story: "She had been running around with her uncle, Gene Heizer, and I thought that she was Gene's girlfriend. Me and Gene was

always big buddies. I was up at the Hilltop Inn. He came up there, and he wanted to ride around. I asked him, 'Who's your girlfriend?' He said, 'That girl with me?' And I said, 'Yeah.' He said, 'Oh, Don, that's Jake and Geneva's girl.' We met in July and married in March on her birthday. And I might as well tell her age. She was fifteen the day that we got married. And we've been married forty-seven years. We've had our ups and downs, but we've had a good life."

On my second visit to the Williamses, later in the summer, they opened a shed door to reveal their onion harvest spread out on makeshift shelves and hanging in bunches from the rafters and nails along the walls. I had never seen so many onions. Referring to them by names such as "potato onions" and "winter onions," Gloria explained how she uses them in

her cooking. For example, the "potato onion," her favorite, is versatile: it shines when eaten raw accompanying soup beans or cooked in a pot of vegetable soup. Once the onions are dried, the Williamses move them into their basement, banking on them lasting until spring. As with most of what they eat, the Williamses do not buy onions at the store. Gloria estimated that they raise 90 percent of their food. They even grow "bread" corn. Don still grinds the meal using the mill that Gloria's father once used. They like Boone County White, but their favorite is Tennessee Red Cob. Don cures his own hams. "Old-fashioned salt cure," he tells me. And the art of making mincemeat is not lost in this household. Gloria remembers how her mother made it, and she has kept the practice alive. "You use the pieces [of the hog] you can't eat, and that's usually the head. You cook the head. You grind that meat. And then you use your homemade [blackberry] jam and your cooked dried apples. You just mix it to the consistency you want, and then you can put it into jars and water-bath it so it will seal." Making mincemeat is easy, to hear Gloria tell it. Because she would never boast, she modestly fails to mention that to prepare this recipe, one would also need to raise the hog, pick blackberries, make jam, grow apples, dry the apples, and own a meat grinder and know how to use it.

Some people might think that Gloria and Don are behind the times or standing still in time or just somehow ill-timed. But the knowledge they have might more rightfully be considered as "just in time." They switched to organic gardening in the late 1990s. Reaching back in time, they use horse manure to enrich their soil just as their parents did, and Don handpicks the bugs for "hours at a time." When Gloria tells me that they are active members of a simple-living group that meets once a month to share food and ideas, I silently wonder why: Gloria and Don seem to have written the book on simple living. But Gloria sets me straight. "We teach each other. We have people from Lexington, Richmond, the University at Morehead, doctors, lawyers. We've made some great friends, people that we would never have met [otherwise], I'm sure. There's some [people from around here] that thinks we're totally off our rockers. But then, actually, I think, gradually more people are drawn into it. Everything doesn't have to be McDonald's."

Indeed, nothing about Gloria and Don is franchised, uniform, or automated. They are like the onions they grow: layered. You peel one layer and in that act you reveal another layer, then another and another, each one slightly different than the one before it. Finally, you hit the center, the core. Just as the potato onion is planted in the fall and left to multiply by forming new onions around the core bulb, so too do the Williamses share, teach, and practice what they know, allowing their expertise to multiply and spread. And like the "winter" bunching onions that provide something fresh and green during the long months when a garden seems far away, Gloria and Don are simply ahead of their time.

"THE LAND IS GOOD HERE"

Martha Barrios and Adan Nuñez

"I WAS BORN in Mexico. In Michoacan. I lived on a ranch, but I never worked on a farm or ranch, because when I was very small, we moved to the city [of] Uruapan." Adan continued, "[My father] was looking for opportunities to work. [He] sold the land. I was nine years old. In Mexico, it is expensive to grow things, the seeds, [for example,] and when you sell it, you don't make any money. It wasn't advantageous. When I came to this country—I've been here ten years—I had never worked out on a farm. I've always worked at companies." Adan, who was born in 1979, has worked in the production line at Fruit of the Loom, first in Clayton, Georgia, and later at the Jamestown, Kentucky, plant.[67]

"We met in Georgia at Fruit of the Loom," Martha said. Martha grew up in the small town of Jilote in Guanajuato, Mexico. She came to the United States in the late 1990s and along with other family members lived in Clayton. Many of her relatives worked for Fruit of the Loom, as did so many others in that northern Georgia mountain community. Martha was employed at the plant, too, for a short period. In 2006, Fruit of the Loom announced that it would be closing the Clayton plant. Adan, by then a father, fortunately landed a transfer and moved to Kentucky. Martha explained, "He came to Kentucky first, and then he came back and brought [Diana, our daughter, and me]. In the beginning, I didn't like Kentucky. In Georgia I had some family. Here I don't know anyone. Everything was

154

different there from here. I knew a lot of people [in Georgia]. There were a lot of people there from my hometown [in Mexico]. When we came here I felt alone, lonely. I wanted to go back to Georgia."

The Hispanic Gardening Project orchestrated by the Russell County Cooperative Extension intervened in Martha's isolation and loneliness. Her past connection to Fruit of the Loom also proved beneficial. In Georgia, Martha had met Marisol Ortiz, who was married to a Fruit of the Loom industrial engineer. Marisol, a native of Puerto Rico, had also moved to Russell County because her husband, like Adan, had been offered a transfer from the Clayton plant. Marisol was involved in the Cooperative Extension's project both as a gardener and as an interpreter.[68] Martha said, "[Marisol] invited me to go work at the garden. And that's how we started going to the garden. I became more calm about being here, less sad. That's where I met Pam, Julie, Wanda, and everybody."[69]

Unlike Adan, Martha had some experience growing a vegetable garden. She had nine siblings, and often, as children, they were sent to help their uncle in his garden. "He grew tomatoes, tomatillos, chilis, cilantro, lettuce, [and other vegetables]," Martha said. "He would sell his vegetables. We would work with him, and he would pay us, but he'd also give us some [produce] to take home with us." I asked her what her earliest memory was of working in her uncle's garden. She answered, "When I was ten years old, I remember weeding. I liked it." She laughed. Then we all laughed like people who know the secret handshake of Weeders Anonymous—those people who find satisfaction in doing work that most people consider tedious, at best, and odious, at worst.

In their weed-free Russell County garden, Adan and Martha grew tomatoes, tomatillos, cucumbers, zucchini, cilantro, chili peppers (habaneros, jalapenos, and poblanos), bell peppers, sweet potatoes, watermelons, cantaloupes, corn, and carrots. They came to the community garden project to understand how to cultivate vegetables, but they were equally curious about how to preserve what they grew.

Teaching gardeners how to put up food, and how to do it safely according to the U.S. Department of Agriculture's standards, was one of the goals of the Hispanic Gardening Project. A household's food security can be greatly increased when the harvest, above what is consumed fresh, is preserved. The gardeners involved in the Russell County project were enthusiastic and prolific food preservationists. But canning, in particular, was a new concept to these gardeners, because they mostly came from climates where the growing season, and thus access to fresh, local produce, was year-round. Home canning was not a necessary practice. However, as new Kentuckians living in a climate where freezing temperatures prevail about five months of the year, they embraced a preservation method that once was commonplace among U.S. rural families.

I asked Martha how many quart jars of tomatoes she had canned. She answered, "About one hundred!" Martha had plenty of tomatoes to last through the winter and probably some to spare. This is important because tomatoes are essential to Mexican cuisine. Plus, she knows how they were grown and how they were preserved. Those one hundred jars of

home-canned, homegrown tomatoes augmented the food security of the Barrios-Nuñez household. And tomatoes are only part of the family's strategy. Martha also canned, froze, and pickled other vegetables. She even put up pinto beans they grew using the Cooperative Extension's pressure canner. Adan estimated, "Almost all the food we'll eat this winter will come from what we grew, except for the meats and the spices and flour." Martha interjected, "It will make a very big difference."

Immigrants to Kentucky—going all the way back to the late eighteenth century—have wanted land here upon which to build their lives. Adan and Martha are no different. "I'd like to have a farm [someday]," Adan said. I asked, "In Kentucky?" He said, "Why not? The land is good here. I like Kentucky." He continued, "We'd raise chickens, goats, [and] sheep. I like farm-fresh eggs. And homegrown chickens taste better." Working in the community garden has made them feel more like Kentuckians, they told me. Their prospects seem bright. "Now when I go to Georgia, I don't want to be there," Martha said. "I want to come back to Kentucky." Spoken like a true Kentuckian.

THE END OF THE ROAD OUT HERE

Valeria and Paul Riley

RAISING A GARDEN is not for the faint of heart. Planting a seed requires faith. The rain might not come soon enough to provide the necessary moisture for germination. Or the seed could wash away in a torrent before it takes hold. But even after a gully washer, some seeds usually do make it, though the survivors may form a wayward row, nothing like the precise one that the gardener intended. Planting habits and desires from one generation to the next also requires conviction, and not unlike what occurs with vegetable seeds, the results may be unforeseen, a new path never imagined. Young people often strike out on their own seeking new experiences, or sometimes they want to harbor the old ways but with alterations. Conversely, older people can change course to take up a mantle dropped in youth. Or their ideas and priorities once set in stone are somehow dislodged. Paul and Valeria Riley's lives have been shaped by these dynamics; their destiny has been formed by those who rejected rural life and those who sought to sustain it. If the Rileys were seeds planted just before a big storm, they might have ended up in crooked garden rows. But the seedlings gone awry are often the toughest of all.

Paul was four years old when he moved to town, with his parents and two brothers, leaving the 235-acre ridgetop farm in Kenton County that had been continuously owned and tended by his father's family since the 1880s. Paul's uncles had already dispersed to California and to nearby

Cincinnati and Covington, but his father, Lawrence, stayed on the farm. As a young man, Lawrence Riley helped his parents—Paul's grandparents—with their enterprise: raising a garden and tobacco along with crops to feed their hogs, cattle, and horses. After serving in the military during World War II, Lawrence returned home, met Paul's mother, Imogene, in nearby Newport, got married, and started a family. Imogene came from farming people, too, but her family's homeplace near Clarksville, Tennessee, had given way to a cluster of family houses, and the farming was, as Paul said, "phased out."

Though their desire may have been strong to stay on the farm, in 1954 the young Riley family, which would eventually grow to seven children, left for better economic opportunities in Covington, only fifteen miles away from the farm. Paul said, "Out of all his brothers, [my father] was probably the one who actually had some real desire to keep in touch and come back to the farm with some frequency. This is where we would come for vacation during the summer. We came to the farm. Me and my older brother, when we got out of school, we would come out here and spend a couple of weeks with my grandmother."

Paul's grandmother, Nannie, was a daughter of Edward Mills. According to Paul, who has researched his family history and maintains much of the family archive, Edward, along with his mother, Susan, and brother, John, were enslaved and living on the farm at the time of the Civil War. They lived in a log house that today is still part of the farm. Paul has never been able to document how this small family—his ancestors—gained ownership of the piece of land with the log house that was the heart of the original farm. Sometimes freed slaves were deeded land by their former owners, so it is possible that the Edward Mills farm had its beginnings in such a transaction. But after Emancipation and as he grew into adulthood, Edward began to accrue adjoining parcels of land, as shown by recorded deeds. Remarkably, by 1889, less than twenty-five years after slavery ended, he had created a good-sized farm of at least three hundred contiguous acres.[70]

"When [Edward] passed," Paul said, "he gave each one of his [nine] children a plot of ground out of the entire estate."[71] With several family homes on the land, he left parcels with houses to two of his daughters because Edward thought they would stay on the farm. He predicted well, because Nannie, Paul's grandmother, and her sister, Alice, lived out their lives on the farm at the end of the road. "But then after [my grandmother] passed [in 1958,] everything kind of fell apart," Paul explained. Paul's father would come out, and they would try to have a garden and even hold family reunions. "That all stopped, too." Paul's grandfather left the farm and "went to town" because he had "too many memories." A cousin, Howard Cummins, who was Alice's son, remained on the farm. He continued to raise tobacco and held the farm together, keeping it from passing out of the family.[72] But the farm life that Paul had known as a boy ended. Still, in his heart and mind, he kept a "desire," as he put it, to be on the farm and tend it. He bided his time.

Valeria, Paul's wife, was born in Stonega, a southwestern Virginia coal camp owned by Westmoreland Coal. Her grandfather was a miner, but his son, her father, wanted a different life for himself and his family. In 1957, when Valeria was seven years old, her parents, Johnny and Olla Weatherspoon, migrated to Cincinnati. Thousands of other black and white families left the coalfields in the 1950s and early 1960s because the coal business had gone bust. Like Valeria's parents, many headed toward midwestern cities where good jobs were available. Because she was an only child and both her parents worked, Valeria explained that "every summer [she] had to catch a train or a bus and go to Virginia to stay with [her] grandparents." She said, "My grandmother was a stay-at-home housewife. That was her job. She raised a garden in her backyard [and] grew corn, peanuts, collard greens, mustard greens—all types of greens, green beans, tomatoes, pickles. She was a canner. She preserved and made jams and jellies. They had a grape [arbor]. She would make wine. There were a few chickens." Valeria continued. "Mainly [I] helped her pick vegetables. I wasn't good with the hoeing. Most of the vegetables were planted by the time I got there, because I didn't go, like I said, until after school was out." But these girlhood summers spent with her grandparents in the place that her parents had had to leave created a "desire" in Valeria that would surface again when she was a young woman.

"I don't know how it happened, but we got into an argument. We was fussing," Paul said. He was explaining the circumstances that had led him and Valeria to make a garden together, before they were married, right in the spot where their house now sits on Edward Mills's farm. "So I was driving. It was late at night. We're arguing but we're trying to talk it out, too. So I keep driving. In my mind, I know where I'm going. We ended up out here. But we didn't come all the way back [to the end of the road]. We stopped at the mailboxes. And she said, 'Where are you taking me?'" Paul continued, "We'd never been out here before." Sitting in country darkness, on top of a ridge, Paul told Valeria about his family and the history of the farm. His story must have been compelling, because they started raising a garden together and then married in 1974 after three and half years of courtship.

Paul and Valeria had met in 1971 after he came home from serving in the U.S. Army, including a year in Vietnam. He had graduated from high school in 1967. He said, "I didn't know what I wanted to do. I just knew I wanted to get out of school and find me a decent job. I didn't have any desire for college. I had never thought about it and never prepared for it. I landed a job in Cincinnati at Proctor and Gamble." When he was drafted into military service two years into his job, the company held the position for him. Paul worked there for thirty-five years as a pipe fitter. In the meantime, Valeria had studied at the University of Cincinnati and earned her degree as a radiologic technician. Later she entered an apprentice electrician program and worked in the building trades for eighteen years. Initially, Valeria and Paul made their home in Covington, but by 1978 they had started a family, built a home on the farm, and moved there permanently. Each day Paul and Valeria, along with their children, Alicia and Kevin, drove into "town" for work and school. They dropped the kids off at Valeria's mother's house in Cincinnati in the early morning before going to work. Olla then would see them off to school. In the late afternoon the Riley family crossed the Ohio River for the second time in one day but now heading south, to make their way home to the farm in Kenton County. The two-hour daily commute was a testament of their fidelity to the farm. And keeping a garden each year was another.

The farm became a central gathering place for their extended families. Valeria explained that she loves to cook, so the Rileys hosted "great family functions." Valeria did much of the cooking and was equally interested in presentation. Family members would ask her to make this dish or that one. The word spread, and their friends would ask her to make their favorite recipe. "It just snowballed," Valeria said. "I got into catering. I had finished working, but Paul [hadn't]. I said, 'I'll try the catering to keep myself busy.'" But when Paul retired in 2004 Valeria quit catering, and together they turned to raising a larger, more organic, more diverse garden that extended from spring through fall. Paul said, "I've always had a desire to have a store where I could sell my own produce. [Valeria] always

had a desire to have a store that she could cater out of. We never got it together." They compromised and began to grow enough excess beyond their own needs to sell at the Covington Farmers Market. In this project, Valeria and Paul were again taking cues from Paul's great-grandfather: Edward Mills peddled vegetables from the farm to a Covington market at the turn of the previous century.

"We try to raise enough of a variety to make the market stand look appealing," Paul said. "We grow tomatoes, green beans, corn, cabbage, squash, eggplants, okra, watermelon. The first year we tried this, I put out one thousand tomato plants. That's not a lot of tomato plants compared to other farmers, but it was a lot of work for two people. We learned that you don't have to put out a whole lot of things, but put out what you can handle and have good-looking quality produce." Even though the two of them have raised a garden for years, they have learned new techniques by attending classes taught by the Kenton County Cooperative Extension and Kentucky State University. Valeria has pushed them toward organic methods and heirloom vegetables. Paul said, "We're not organic [yet]. We don't use any herbicides at all, we try not to use any chemical insecticides. All the insecticides we use are Bt and neem.[73] We try to use some organic fertilizers." Valerie interjected, "I'm trying to compost." Paul added, "Next year is going to be a ground-building year for us. The conferences we go to—the first thing they tell you is to have your ground enriched to the point that you don't need to fertilize, where you don't need to use insecticides. We kind of saw that this year in our compost heap. There were tomatoes and squash that came up [in the compost pile]. Not once did bugs bother it. Some of the prettiest squash. It made a believer of me."

Valeria and Paul own land that the former slave, Edward Mills, labored to acquire after the Civil War. His feat may be why Valeria and Paul are not taking any chances: they employ many of the most modern, sustainable agricultural methods to restore Mills's legacy to healthy and productive ground. They are stewards, not merely owners. One of Paul's cousins, who grew up on the farm and is the granddaughter of Edward, whom she calls "Dad," told Paul, "Dad sure would have been proud of you, all you've done. Even if you had had to put up a lien to keep the farm, he would have been proud. He definitely would have been proud of where you are today, with the gardening and all."

Sustaining land goes hand in hand with caring for self and community. Valeria explained, "[Gardening] is a relaxing time for me to get out, to work, and plant the vegetables and care for the vegetables. You have time to meditate. It is a carefree atmosphere. If you are stressed out, it helps to relieve the stress. So to me it is therapy." Paul said, "It is an accomplishment to me when you put something in the ground [and] watch it grow, you keep it nice and pretty, cultivated. And it produces this product that is going to give you some nourishment, feed you. That is unique. And when you can say you did that, that is a true accomplishment." But personal achievement and self-satisfaction, while perhaps necessary to our mental health, are alone not enough for Paul and Valeria. Paul built a potting shed for Valeria that they hope will double as a laboratory and classroom. They plan to bring children out to the farm to teach them how to garden. "Not just black kids," Paul explained, "just kids in general, because it's not just that black kids have lost touch [with growing food]—everybody has. Young people come to the market, and their first question is, 'How do I prepare these green beans?' And your first thought is, 'Are they serious?' That's what we've lost."

It is true. Much has been lost, including the majority of three generations of the Edward Mills family who left the farm. Paul allows that he and Valeria had a particular set of economic circumstances that permitted them to keep the farm, live on it, and work to rebuild its vitality. They recognize that as African Americans this is no small accomplishment. Paul said, "I only know of one other African American family in northern Kentucky who still farm. To be lucky enough that [this land] has been passed down from generation to generation to generation and still be in our family, [well], I say to myself that we have been blessed to the point that we

can do that. It has been hard work, but I was blessed with a decent job that allowed us the privilege to keep the farm another generation." And in the process they have managed to bring family and friends more frequently to the farm—if only for a summer's afternoon—to create the extended community that Paul and Valeria were seeking.

"You don't realize how what we've been doing brings everyone together," Paul said. He believes that families in the past were closer, especially those living in rural spaces. "I think it is because a large portion of our society lived off the land. You shared that. [It] made you closer . . . and that is what I see out here. And the last couple of years we've had so many people coming out here to buy. We didn't make it to the market this year at all.[74] We signed up for two markets, and every time we thought we had enough stuff to get us there, we'd start getting telephone calls from people who wanted to come out and buy some things. The corn was sold before I picked it. The potatoes were sold before I dug them." Their customers are family and friends from the Cincinnati area, including people they have become acquainted with at the Covington Farmers Market. Yes, their visitors want fresh vegetables, Paul said, but they also want to "sit under the maple tree" and talk. "It means a lot to me," Paul explained. "Family and friends. If that is what gardening does, then I'm happy with that."

The maple tree represents a piece of history. To be able to sit under it symbolizes an even larger slice. When Paul's father moved his young family to Covington and left the farm he loved, it may be, paradoxically, that very move which saved the bulk of Edward Mills's farm. Paul said that his father "worked hard trying to keep [the farm] so he could pass it down to his kids," and Paul is "trying to continue that." Neither of Paul and Valeria's two children seems interested in pursuing a rural life or even gardening, a situation that Paul qualified with a hopeful "not yet." But there is a niece, the daughter of Paul's sister, in Washington, DC, who gardens and wants to study agriculture in college.

The Edward Mills farm has seen people come and go. Some left because their aspirations could not be achieved by a life at the end of the road. Others stayed the course and held the line. Paul and Valeria have done both in order to nurture and protect the farm and to keep the land in their family. When Paul said, "Now what happens after us, I can't do anything about," I heard a combination of a lament and a question, mixed with a guarded faith. He and Valeria know that they need just one person to emerge—someone fearless who will plant a seed and stick around to watch it grow.

"RAISED TO WORK"

Betty Decker

"I WAS BORN in 1948, and there were twelve of us children," Betty said. "And everybody had a certain job to do. We were told maybe once what to do, but after that we knew what our jobs were, and we just done it. Daddy and Mama always had a large garden, and everybody [had to work in it]. If we ate, we worked, and if we didn't work and contribute to a meal," Betty paused but then continued, "I mean, we had to work. And I'm glad. I'm glad that we was raised to work. I remember one time my grandmother came down to visit us, and they were two or three little kids in the house that wasn't in the garden. And my grandmother said to my mother, 'Where is the other three?'" Betty's mother answered, "They're in the house." Betty's grandmother responded, "Go fetch those kids out here. If they're not big enough to use a hoe, they can drag one."

The garden of Betty's girlhood was a typical one for that time and place. She grew up on Rocky Branch in Wayne County, in south-central Kentucky. The garden was large by today's standards, somewhere between an acre and a half and two acres, and was located just beyond the yard. Using a tractor, her father plowed the garden, then used a disc harrow to further break up the soil to ready it for planting.[75] Afterward, the garden became her mother's domain, with the children providing additional labor. Her father owned multiple farms, tending several hundred acres of land, in addition to their homeplace. He logged timber and raised cattle, hogs, tobacco, and hay and owned a few horses. Betty said, "Daddy never bought any hay." Nor did her mother buy any vegetable seeds. She saved her seeds from year to year, carefully drying them on a cloth and putting them in jars that contained "some strong [hot] pepper to keep the bugs out of the seed," Betty explained. In each jar Betty's mother placed a slip of paper upon which she had written in pencil the name of the seed. Naturally, the seeds she saved reflected what she grew in her garden: tomatoes, cabbage, lettuces, onions, corn, yellow squash, peppers, cornfield beans, melons, popcorn, peanuts, cucumbers, peas, and, their revered family bean, the "Granny Bell stick bean."[76]

During the 1950s, Betty's family practiced subsistence agriculture, an economic and cultural strategy that had been dramatically declining in Kentucky following World War II. Neither of her parents worked for wages at what rural people often called a "public works job." Instead the family lived by a perfected household economy combined with cash derived from a tobacco crop, small-scale logging, and the sale of cattle and hogs not needed for the family's use. Betty's father used much of that money to buy more land and pay property taxes. According to Betty, they were not unusual in their community. "What we done, everybody else done," she said. Perhaps, though, Betty's family remained more completely immersed in these older forms of livelihood, because Betty noticed differences between her family and a few of the other children in her one-room school. Some children brought for lunch processed meats or peanut butter, foods that were likely purchased at a store. "One family brought a soda for lunch, and that really looked good to me," Betty said. Another vivid memory was a "girl [who] had a can of potted meat and crackers for her lunch" and gave Betty a taste of the meat. She remembered it as "the best-tasting stuff" and in stark contrast to the food she and her siblings took for their lunch: leftovers from breakfast that morning or from supper the night before. There was also one family in their community who "would take their children to school." Betty said, "I thought they were so lucky." She continued, "But when I think about it, we were the lucky ones." To reach school she and her siblings only had to walk across their father's fields. "I can look back now and it was just a precious thing."

As is true of many children, even obedient ones, Betty occasionally tried to shirk her work, especially in the garden. When she was four or five, one of her first jobs in her mother's garden was to plant seeds evenly spaced in a furrow. "We were told and showed how to drop them, how far apart to put the seed and not waste [the seed]," Betty remembered. This is how all the younger children started working in the garden. Betty said that she plotted about what she could do to lessen her load. "I thought, well now, mother will never notice this, and I get so tired of planting. And I'd just put them really thick, [thinking] I'll be done quicker." Laughing, Betty admitted that she did get finished sooner but then, she said, "Mama would check and then I'd have to go back and pick all the seed up where it was too thick." By the time she was a teenager, Betty had learned to hoe, set plants, harvest crops, and assist with canning and freezing.

"I hated it, and at that time I thought I would never, ever have a garden of my own. Hot and sweaty and backbreaking. I mean there was no breaks. You hit the garden at daylight and stayed there till dark, nearly. We done it because we were told to do it. [But] one time I remember me and my mother was working in the garden. Everybody else was off in the fields, in the cornfields or tobacco. We had worked all day. We hadn't stopped to eat no lunch or nothing, and I'd asked my mother to stop and take a little break. She said, 'We can't take a break. We've got to get this garden worked.' So I decided I was going to take a break with or without my mother. I regret that now. It was down in the evening, for the shade was coming over an old corncrib that was up at the barn. And I thought, I'm going up there and sit in the shade of that crib and rest just for a few minutes. Well, when I went up there I started to turn around and sit down, and this big black snake stuck its head out of that crib, and you know the first person I hollered for to come kill that snake? My mother. So Mama come and killed the snake and back to the garden we went."

This tale with its moral and even biblical overtones is an important marker to Betty. When she told me the story she also said, "But when I got married, I've had a garden every year. I just felt like I had to grow a garden in order to have something to eat." While Betty's economic health may not depend on her garden in the way her mother's did, her internal state does. Betty seems to relish doing things the way her mother did. It is important for her to carry on the traditions, the old ways, to hold on when so much around her has changed. "You know, I raised my children a lot like Mother did. I grew a garden like she did, and I just do about everything the same way that my parents did." Betty has added her own innovations, however. She loves her rototiller, for instance, and believes in mulching. No more hoeing! She starts her plants with a hydroponic system she refers to as "water beds." She made a raised bed for her strawberries so that she did not have to stoop as much while picking them. And she does not grow peanuts, because "that's too much work," but she does grow broccoli, cauliflower, Brussels sprouts, and zucchini—vegetables that were not in her mother's repertoire.

Deciding what is and what is not too much work can be a question of cultural longing and memory as much as it is one about efficiency and cost-effectiveness. Like her mother, Betty still preserves food by canning. She works in her canning house that sits over her root cellar. Her mother had one, too—a building, separate from the main house, with its own cooking stove and a workspace to clean and prepare the fruits and vegetables. After the jars have sealed and cooled, Betty, just as her mother once did, carries them down the steps to the cellar that will protect them from extremes of hot and cold. Betty's cellar is orderly and full. There are rows of tomatoes and tomato juice, grape juice, green beans, relishes, and jams. One item that is not on her shelves is her mother's special "stuffed peppers." "Mama would take these big bell peppers," Betty said, "and she would shred up cabbage and corn, just whatever we liked, and [put the mixture inside the peppers, the tops of which had been carefully cut off,] and then take the top of the pepper and sew—actually sew—the top

back onto the [stuffed pepper] to keep it together." Then two or three peppers per quart jar were processed in a hot water bath. Betty makes stuffed peppers, but she stores them in the freezer, which is much easier, not requiring a needle and thread. But when the family kills a hog, Betty still cans some of the homemade sausage even though that is far more time-consuming than throwing it in the freezer. Betty explained, "Mama always canned sausage, and I like to put up some the way she did it."

In Betty's mind, her mother's life and death are forever connected to the garden. She said, "The saddest thing that I can remember now about gardening [is that] I know my mother must have got so tired. And deep down she had to resent that, too. I mean, she was my mother, but she was human, too. She had to resent that and think, 'Will I ever get all this done?'" Betty continued, clearing her throat, "The last [spring] mother lived, she wanted [her] garden plowed up and turned and she wanted the garden planted. We went ahead and put out a garden that spring, and she wanted that garden taken care of even though I think she knowed that she would never live to be able to eat any of the food that was growed that summer. It was just something that she thought had to be done." She died in May before the summer garden could reach its fullness.

Betty's mother had many more mouths to feed than her daughter ever has. A productive garden was a necessity. But if someone had come from a university to interview her about what gardening meant to her, she would have likely expressed some measure of joy and satisfaction about her lifetime of growing food. Her daughter thinks gardening is good exercise, a worthy way to "occupy" the mind and save money. But Betty also knows it has some less-tangible meaning. "Doesn't it give you a really good feeling, too, when you can stand back and look at all these beautiful plants and say, 'This is mine and I grew it with my own hands and I'm going to can this for my family'? I just really, really enjoy it," Betty declared. "I hope I can garden till the very last." Now in her sixties and taking her mother's place as an elder, Betty has experienced the gratification that comes from a lifetime of work. Garden work can be tedious, repetitive, and hard. Some years the garden yields are prodigious, but in others the lack of rain and presence of pests and disease cause concern about the winter stores. But no matter what, season after season, year after year, garden after garden, it is the work of a life force.

THE FAMILY WHO LIVES IN THE GARDEN

Saunda Richardson Coleman

"I ACTUALLY LIKE TO TALK to my plants," Saunda said. When she comes home from a stressful day at work, visiting her garden is the best antidote. "I know that sounds a little crazy, but for me, [they are] like a little family." Gardeners other than Saunda have been known to speak to plants, and there are those of us who tend and protect our garden as if it were a loved one, but Saunda's willingness to expand the conventional definition of family is probably greater than that of most others. In 1963, when she was two years old, her father, jazz musician Smoke Richardson, died, and by the time she was thirteen her mother, Carol, too, had passed. With no brothers and sisters, Saunda became, in her words, an "orphan."

The association of a garden with loss of family is strong in Saunda's memory. Her father was a saxophonist who led his own Lexington band—Smoke Richardson Orchestra. He was born in Covington, Kentucky, in 1906 and left high school to set out for New York City, where he cut a record. He was twenty-eight years older than his wife and died before their fourth anniversary. To keep his memory alive in her daughter, who was too young to form her own, Carol told Saunda more than once, "Your father loved to be outdoors." He had a rose garden that he tended, but Saunda never learned where his love of the soil originated. She guessed that his late nights playing music caused him to seek the quiet and solace of his garden by day.

176

When Saunda was about five years old, another garden memory was formed. Her mother taught the third grade in Lexington Public Schools. One of her colleagues, Lillian King, took an interest in Saunda and became what Saunda called her "play aunt." "Aunt Lilly" had grown up in Harlan County, Kentucky, in the coal town of Benham. When Lillian went back home to visit her family, she took Saunda with her on several occasions. Lillian's father, William, who kept a beautiful and tidy vegetable garden, often invited Saunda to tend the plot with him. "I remember pulling this huge stalky thing with a round bulb," Saunda said. "It seemed like it was tall as a tree. But it was just an onion."

As they tried to adjust to a life without Smoke, Carol bought a house in a different neighborhood, and they moved to Lexington's West End. This house and its yard were to figure prominently in Saunda's memory as she got older. There, she and her mother gardened in the backyard.

Carol raised tomatoes, while Saunda's choices for her small plot were guided by their neighbor, George Watson, a seasoned gardener. "He handed me a sack of green bean seeds, and he'd show me how to space them. Then when mine would come up, I'd hand him some of my beans over the [fence]. I started loving gardening."

After her mother died, Saunda's "world was turned upside down," emotionally and economically. But her mother's modeling as a schoolteacher helped carry Saunda through high school and college. Upon graduation from Eastern Kentucky University in 1983, she took a job as a telephone operator at the University of Kentucky. When the university offered employees small plots of land on the edge of campus for growing vegetables, Saunda took advantage of the opportunity and raised a garden. And when in 1988 she moved back into her mother's house, where she had exchanged beans with George Watson and the soil was "beautiful and black," she once again began to tend a garden in her own backyard, reconnecting her memory with her practice.

Today Saunda lives with her husband, Tim, and their three large dogs in another part of Lexington. She raises a garden in her front and side yards, since the family pets need the fenced backyard. Rejecting the convention of a backyard garden was easy when Saunda discovered good, rich soil alongside the house. There she grows Brandywine tomatoes, pumpkins, squash, chard, potatoes, onions, Amish deer-tongued lettuce, herbs, and cabbage, including, once, a five-pound head that Tim, who doesn't garden, nevertheless "protected" from marauders. And she raises that cornerstone vegetable of nearly all Kentucky gardens: green beans.

A front-yard garden brought unexpected pleasures for Saunda. She met other vegetable gardeners in her neighborhood because they could easily see her working in her garden. And she meets nongardening neighbors who walk by and stop to look at her edible landscaping. She invites them into her yard/garden because her impulse is always to share. "I love giving my food away. It brings me so much joy," Saunda said. "People come by and say, 'Wow, could we have some?' I have a tomato list now."

And as she plucks a tomato to give to a passerby, she might also take the opportunity to advocate for the benefits of home vegetable gardening. Saunda also exchanges seeds, plants, and ideas with other nearby gardeners. "We all love food. It connects us all." Each time Saunda passes along a plant or gives away a head of cabbage, she is reenacting the times when Aunt Lilly's father invited her into his garden and when Mr. Watson taught her to pass seeds and the fruit they bear over the fence. She is calling forth her father's connection to the outdoors and her mother's tomato patch. She is cultivating family and community along with vegetables and herbs.

Saunda's work with "special needs" children, especially those with autism, is another kind of practice in opening the boundaries between family, community, and garden. Sometimes she works with individual families as a caregiver. Frequently, she shares vegetables from her garden with them, subtly introducing the benefits of gardening to a group of children for whom communication and interaction with stimuli are key. And over time, Saunda encourages and helps these families to make

their own gardens. Autistic children respond particularly well to gardens and gardening, Saunda said. It is "hands-on" work in which the children can express, "Look what I've done!" Saunda believes that they find satisfaction because they have given back by producing something. Even when the children do not work in a garden but simply smell or taste its bounty, the sensory experience is a positive and interactive one, Saunda suggested.

At a camp in Lexington's Castlewood Park, Saunda plants a "therapeutic" garden for children with special needs who participate in a parks and recreation summer program. The campers learn to identify plants by sight, smell, and taste. "I try to plant stuff I think the children will enjoy watching," Saunda said. But when she announces, "Today we're going to eat everything in the garden," there is a near rush even though "a lot of these kids have taste and food problems. They ate leaf lettuce, onions, radishes. Some of them had never tasted anything [fresh]. There's so much we can do with gardening."

That is why there was no confusion for Saunda when she designed her business card. On a violet background with a purple clematis bloom in the foreground, it announces, "Smoke Gardens and Autism Services, Saunda Carol Coleman, Gardener/Special Needs Counselor." She will make a vegetable garden for those who want one but cannot do it themselves for one reason or another. She will care for your autistic loved one, with or without a garden—but preferably *with,* since Saunda believes that "gardening will open up a whole new world for [people]. Gardening is like life. Just when you think nothing is going on, you look down and, oh! It is like finding twenty dollars in your pocket every day. God takes the smallest of things and makes them into something else. Blessings. It is a renewing of life."

It is no wonder that Saunda talks to her plants as if they are family. Her father, mother, play Aunt Lilly, and neighbor George Watson are present in every garden she cultivates. Along the way, she has gathered autistic children and their loved ones into her garden family, too, as well as strangers who walk by her home and contemplate the vegetables in the front yard. Some of us are privileged. We do not have to look far for family. We take it for granted. Saunda has had to reckon with its absence since she was a young girl. But she figured it out: there is always family waiting for her in the garden.

THE WORTH OF A VIEW

Jose Meza

TO MEET JOSE MEZA I first stopped in Nicholasville, the seat of Jessa-mine County, to pick up his sister Marcela. She was going to interpret during our interview, because Jose feels most comfortable speaking in Spanish and I can only speak English. But Marcella also proved to be a good interviewer, intervening at times with evocative questions and sometimes fleshing out Jose's comments and filling in gaps of the family story.

It was early November but a warm enough day for us to sit outside at a picnic table that was still loaded with Jose's *calabaza* harvest.[77] From the table I could see so much: Jose's wife, Juana, working in her cantaloupe-colored kitchen; a corner of Jose's garden where large plastic bags on poles still fluttered even though their summer job as scarecrows was over; a garage filled with equipment used to keep cars on the road and tractors in the field; and, behind me, a 180-degree panorama of farm-land below, reminding me, once again, how the Kentucky landscape can thrill and surprise.[78]

Jose and his thirteen brothers and sisters, including Marcela, grew up in San Francisco de los Romo, a small town in the Mexican state of Aguas-calientes. As the oldest son, Jose worked with his father on a farm, where they grew corn, beans, chili peppers, peaches, and grapes. They did not own the land, nor did they live on it. Whatever was grown on the farm, including in the garden, belonged to the owner. Now in Kentucky, with his

182

own family to support—he and Juana have two daughters and four sons—
Jose has continued his work as a farmer. He raises corn and hay for the
landowner.[79] Initially they lived in Nicholasville, but now the family lives
on the farm, where Jose has raised vegetables for his family since 2006.

As he did with his father, Jose grows corn, beans, and chilis. He aug-
ments those staples with strawberries, melons, cucumbers, squash, and
tomatoes. He buys most of his plants but does save his calabaza seeds,
which were originally gifts from other Mexican gardeners. Juana roasts
tomatoes and chilis before putting them in the freezer for her winter
cooking, though she gently chides her husband for growing too much. He
uses spoiled or old hay—hay that he grew but was leftover at the end of
winter and unusable as feed for stock—to enrich his soil and improve its
tilth. And though he does not like to use pesticides, he buys Sevin at
Walmart and applies it when necessary.

As is true of gardeners everywhere, Jose has his pest peeve: thieves in his corn. "I work for the raccoons," he said. With more mouths to feed, Jose had to increase his corn production. In their own ornery way, the raccoons served as an inspiration for a labor-saving device: Jose designed and fabricated a gasoline-powered cultivator that he uses to keep his garden rows weed free. Made of discarded parts from farm implements, it is colorful and fanciful looking. Red and green, like the Mexican flag, with dashes of yellow on its wheels, the sculptural machine gets the job done. Jose has to work long hours during the growing season to be a successful farmer. When he finishes, he turns to his garden, working until dusk. But every now and then, in the midst of this regimen, Jose also allows himself to have a gardener's dream: he wants to grow an avocado tree in Kentucky. But "the weather is in the way here," he said. Compared to Mexico, the Kentucky growing season is much shorter, Jose explained, and therefore too cold for the frost-sensitive avocado. He also hopes to plant peach and apricot trees like the ones he used to tend in Aguascalientes, an ambition more easily realized than the avocado in the Jessamine County climate.

What Kentucky takes away from Jose's dreams because of its prolonged cold season, it gives back in fertile land, adequate rainfall, and a view. In the summer months, the extended Meza family often gathers at the farm.[80] Marcela said, "Everybody comes on the weekends and just sits by the garden. It reminds us of Mexico." They eat Juana's homemade tortillas and salsa and her tamales, if they are lucky, and share Jose's watermelons or cantaloupes fresh from the garden. And the view is spectacular. Jose said, "En realidad se mira muy lejos. Mira. Ya no en la cuidad." *You can see a really long way from here. Look. We're not in the city anymore.* Marcela offered, "He can breathe better and feel more free." Jose said, "Los pájaros. El aire. Todo." *The birds. The air. All of it.* With all this, the trade for the avocado does not seem like a bad one.

YOU CAN'T BUY A GARDEN,
A GOOD NEIGHBOR, OR A PAST

Bev May

BEV MAY RUNS A HEALTH CLINIC for those with no home or little money in the mountains of eastern Kentucky. Her elderly patients some-times pay her in vegetables or share their seeds saved from last summer's juiciest and largest watermelon. She talks with them about victories and problems in her own creek-side garden, which has a tendency to flood and is easy pickings for deer. With her younger patients, Bev finds herself advocating for the economy of gardening and pushing its added benefits of healthy food and exercise. She moves fluidly from nurse practitioner to vegetable gardener and then back to clinician. Like a steward, Bev is tending to people and land as if they mattered.

When I met Bev in the mid-1980s, she was a nursing student at the University of Kentucky who was working with Lexington activists to pass a constitutional amendment outlawing the broad form deed in Kentucky, a movement spearheaded by a group then known as Kentucky Fair Tax Coali-tion (KFTC).[81] Bev was central because she had been a KFTC organizer, was from the eastern Kentucky coalfields, and was an engaging speaker and passionate advocate for the cause. I had always remembered Bev's warmth, intelligence, and gift of gab. Surely Bev was a gardener, I thought. I wrote her. She claimed that it was "a reassurance to be suspected of gardening." She told me that she looked forward to describing her "weird experiments" and "supply[ing] comic relief" for my project. I do not know about "comic relief," but on the January day when I visited her Floyd County home on Wilson Creek, near Maytown, the stories poured from her.

She grows her garden on land that her grandmother, Trilby May, once cultivated. Sitting under the shade of a box elder tree, Bev spent her girlhood summers during the 1960s and early '70s shelling peas or breaking up beans while listening to Mama Trilby tell stories. Bev's mother and Bradis, her mother's mother, who lived on the other side of the mountain separating Wilson Creek from Hog Hollow, were also part of the audience. "If I would just keep my hands busy at breaking beans and not be noticed, then the talk would get a good deal more interesting and rich," Bev told me. By being still and listening, Bev learned about the history of her community and the rhythms and strategies of good storytelling. I saw her eyes light up as she remembered one of Mama Trilby's most delicious stories. "There was a terrible problem with syphilis before World War II around here because a lot of menfolk would go and work in the log woods or go work in the gas fields. And they would come back and give their women syphilis. It was an epidemic." Bev paused and, like all good storytellers, alerted me with a facial expression that the story was about to take a turn. "My grandmother started naming names." Bev, whose presence had been forgotten, listened as Mama Trilby identified all the women who had syphilis in the 1920s and 1930s. Then, mixing the remembered shock of the small child with the adult sense of a good story, Bev concluded, "These [were] women who I knew as elder pillars of the church."

Mama Trilby also looms large in Bev's development as a gardener. She subscribed to *Organic Gardening* even though, as Bev wryly put it, "she was an organic gardener who used Sevin dust."[82] Bev pored over her grandmother's old issues gleaning "information" and "inspiration." Also influential was a course she took at Morehead State University called "Population, Resources, and Environment," a class in which the effects of DDT were discussed.[83] The late 1970s, the period in which Bev was an undergraduate, saw the environmental movement strengthen in the United States. As Bev explained, "There was a lot of distrust for the chemical companies, [like] Monsanto, [who] had sold us this bill of goods about [how] you can't garden or farm without chemicals. That was all being brought into question by the back-to-the-landers."[84]

After graduating with a psychology degree but unable to find a job in eastern Kentucky, Bev lived at home for a brief period. She tried substitute teaching and experimented with French intensive gardening, a method of double-digging to prepare a deeply cultivated bed that allows for more densely spaced plantings. That year a flood in the late spring washed out her garden, and "to add insult to injury one of the trees on the creek bank fell over on top of [it]." Bev took it as a sign that she needed to leave eastern Kentucky to find a job. She headed for Seattle, where she had made friends on a trip the year before. Quickly she found a job working in the downtown YWCA's domestic abuse shelter for women. By her own description, she was a "hayseed, a country kid in the middle of a large growing city" participating in an ongoing "cultural comedy." Bev, who has a storyteller's ability to laugh at herself, told me that one of the most "embarrassing" encounters was when she "admitted a transvestite to the shelter." She recalled, "I didn't realize that she was a he. I thought she was awfully tall, but it never entered my mind that anyone [who] had on women's clothes wouldn't be a woman." At other times, though, it was not Bev but those around her who missed the cues. She did try to garden in Seattle, because, as she put it, making a garden in the spring of the year is, for her, a "compulsion." She also found familiar greens such as dandelion in her backyard, picked them, and to the shock of her housemates "made a pot of greens." Still laughing and with her eyes sparkling, Bev concluded, "It was a scandal that I would be actually eating something that grew in the backyard. Of course, when you have a compulsion in a different cultural context, it looks puzzling to other people." Indeed, either being a transvestite or cooking a pot of spring greens has its own cultural logic.

Bev took a hiatus from gardening after leaving Seattle and going home to Kentucky. But once she had completed her nursing degree and secured a job at Eula Hall's model Mud Creek Health Clinic, not far from where she had grown up, she began gardening again in a "postage stamp" plot provided by her landlord. It was in this garden that Bev began to understand that good neighbors could enrich one's gardening knowledge as well as one's arsenal of good stories. This first garden, all her own, apart from her family's land, was also where she began to experiment in earnest. In due time, her neighbor, Guy, a beekeeper and gardener in his early eighties, befriended Bev. Another neighbor who kept a big garden next to Guy's also took an interest in her new young neighbor. "I guess they took pity on [me for] the little postage stamp and said, 'Would you like to split garden space with us?'" Without hesitation, Bev accepted. With her new roomy garden beckoning, she planted potatoes, beans, eggplants, different kinds of peppers, tomatoes, and more greens than she could eat. And her best friend surprised her with a nearly life-size cement pig as a campy garden ornament. Bev was in, well, hog heaven. That year she experimented with growing Bantam corn, an old-time variety that reaches only five to six feet tall and forms short but sweet ears. Near her corn was Guy's "gorgeous Silver Queen towering to the skies," she said. "So like a good neighbor he shows up with a sack of Silver Queen corn. He reaches it over the fence, and he says, 'Here's some corn. It didn't look like yours was turning out too good. But now if this is tough you can feed it to your *hog.*'"

For Bev, "part of the joy of having a good garden is having good neighbors." Now that she is back living on Wilson Creek, back to the place where Mama Trilby once held court, neighbors continue to be a sustaining force. She built her house on the spot once occupied by the family's barn and cows. During construction, Bev installed a chain-link fence with a gate to prevent people from, as she explained, "packing off my building materials, [since] usually nobody [was] on site except evenings and weekends." Once the house was finished, she removed the fence. But her neighbor Treena who lives farther up Wilson Creek had her eye on the fence. Treena's mother called Bev's mother to ask, "What's Beverly gonna do with that fence that she's taken out? Tell her that Treena would like to buy it, 'cause she can put it around her horses." Bev explained that this is how business is done—"the mommies are in contact with each other."

Bev had her mother call back and say, "I don't want to sell it, but I will barter the fence for a load of horse manure." The bargain was struck, and Treena carted off the fencing. Later, while Bev was enjoying the sun on the deck at the back of her new house, she thought she heard some commotion, but by the time she got out front the source of the noise was gone. She realized what had taken place when she saw a large pile of manure near her driveway and learned that her friend Randy had been cleaning out Treena's barn with a front-end loader. The next time Bev saw him she asked, "Did you leave a load of shit in my yard?"

With her garden's nutritional problems solved for the time being, Bev soon had a more complicated challenge: her garden is actually across the road *and* the creek from her house. Her access to it is over a little bridge and through a gate controlled by a neighbor, although the common understanding is that the strip of land is part of the old county road. But the neighbors, who began living for weeks at a time in Lexington, started locking the gate. Bev could not get to her sizable garden with any equipment to plow or cultivate. With her organizer's skills still intact, Bev started talking

to her other neighbors to see whether there might be a collective solution. The first neighbor, who lives at the mouth of the hollow, told her it was "no problem at all" that she should take the equipment through his front yard and head up the hollow. The next neighbor showed her where to go through his land, and before she could even finish the story, he told her, "You gotta be able to get to your garden." Bev mused about their generosity. "This year I realized how important it is to have neighbors, not neighbors as people that live next door but neighbors that you can cooperate with and that can help each other out. Because if you start thinking about it, it took a neighbor with a front-end loader, a neighbor with horses, and two neighbors with property to get the garden this year."

This cooperative spirit rooted in the history of knowing a place and living together in a place has also saved this place. Wilson Creek was slated for mountaintop removal by Miller Brothers Coal in 2006. In this most rapacious method of surface mining, mountains are literally blown up to get to the coal seam. Everything but the coal is shoved elsewhere, including into watersheds. The land can never be put back together as it once was. Water, soil, trees, rocks, wildlife, plants, people, families, communities, and ancient and more recent ecologies are profoundly uprooted, if not destroyed. Since the broad form deed was declared illegal in Kentucky in 1988—because of the hard work of Bev and many others—coal companies now must gain permission from landowners to mine. Cooperation and community ties or the lack of them can mean everything in a situation like the one that Wilson Creek residents face. "If you went on up the holler, there's a big fork," Bev said. "That's the place where Miller Brothers is intending to start a big mountaintop removal job. I've been in communication with those families up there quite a lot. There're two elderly couples that made the decision that they're not going to sign, they not going to let their property be mined no matter what. They're real important to the rest of us, because they're staving it off." Bev cannot resist pointing out that these families keep large gardens, too. In addition to reaching a critical and strategic mass of landowners who refuse to give

Miller Brothers Coal permission to mine, many neighbors contributed to a "Lands Unsuitable for Mining" (LUM) petition. After an initial victory in lower courts, the LUM decision was overturned by the Kentucky Court of Appeals. But that decision came after the coal industry was in a downward economic cycle. For now Wilson Creek is safe.

The survival of Wilson Creek is far more than a political challenge to Bev. This place and her garden are what connect her to the past. This is her lifeblood. Mama Trilby sitting under the box elder tree so many years ago shelling peas and telling stories is only part of it. Bev explained to me what she claimed she "didn't have any good words for." She said, tenderly, "To know I'm in my great-grandmother's cornfield is just the most wonderful feeling. I realized the first year that I started turning up the ground for a garden that there are no rocks. It's very rare that I come across a rock, because all the generations that came before me have already thrown those rocks out in the creek. They did that work for me. So what I have is this wonderful gift of a good piece of ground that was ready to be a garden. You can't buy that."

THE LESSON OF *NHAN* AND *HONG*

Thai Tran

"MY HOUSE WAS MADE of coconut leaves and dirt. We had a very big yard in the back and front [with] creeks running around the house. I remember one time we got in [the creek] and tried to catch shrimp. On other days, I'd tie coconut flowers to a thread and fish for little crabs for fun." Thai Tran remembers, too, a large longan tree in the yard. It produced a favorite traditional fruit that the Vietnamese call *nhan*. These are some of Thai's only memories of the family homeplace in his native Vietnam.

He was born in the province of Ben Tre in the Mekong Delta in 1984, the youngest of ten children.[85] By the time he was five years old, after a short stay with an aunt in Saigon and six months in the Philippines, Thai, his parents, and four brothers and four sisters arrived in Louisville, Kentucky. His oldest sister stayed behind.[86] The family, sponsored by Catholic Charities, moved into the Americana Apartments in the south end of the city, where the Vietnamese community remains concentrated today. As Thai told me, "We lived in two apartments actually—because we had such a big family—right next to each other. Nobody knew English in my family, so I basically taught myself. I struggled throughout elementary school [to learn English]."

Thai's first impulse to grow vegetables occurred during his first few years at the Americana Apartments. He said, "I saw an onion and it had started sprouting. An onion from the store in a bag. I got some dirt from outside, put it in a pot, planted it." A few years later, when Thai was eight years old, the family bought a house in the same neighborhood. His parents started a vegetable garden in the backyard. They dug it up with shovels, added 10-10-10 fertilizer, and grew *rau muon* (water spinach), *muop* (edible luffas), *bau* (bottle brush gourd), and *kho qua* (bitter melon), along with Thai basil, an essential ingredient in Vietnamese cuisine. Thai's parents were not skilled farmers who wanted to continue a tradition from their past. In Vietnam, even in the more rural Mekong Delta, all these vegetables were readily available at local markets. They could also be found at an Asian grocery in Louisville but were rarely fresh. Thai explained that his parents did not have to already know how to garden, because a "common knowledge" existed. "Everybody knows everybody [in the Vietnamese community,] and the word passes around. They give you plants and [share seeds]. They don't really have a method. If they have a plant, they put it into the dirt. If it is a climbing plant, they build a trellis for it." And so, these new Kentuckians cultivated their traditional Vietnamese vegetables by the same means that many long-time Kentuckians have used: knowledge "passed from one person to another" in the oral tradition.

About the time that Thai was mastering English at Rutherford Elementary, he was befriended by an experienced gardener. Thai became interested in a backyard garden that he walked by each day going to and from school. In the garden, which was visible from the sidewalk, he could also see a man working. The older man and Thai started talking to each other. The gardener's name, Thai would learn, was Charlie Moore. Thai said, "[H]e educated me about gardening. He gave me sunflower seeds and told me to plant them. They weren't successful. He told me to try again. He gave me tomatoes and turnips [and] a bird-gourd house." Charlie taught Thai how to identify vegetable plants, when to water and fertilize, and how to build tomato cages from the wire mesh used to reinforce concrete. And, Thai said laughing, "I would get a pop every day, too. I am still friends with him. His hair is white as can be, and he has it all slicked back like an old-time farm boy. I love him."

Tradition underpins Thai's life and the garden he now keeps with his wife and fellow gardener, Jacinda. His parents taught him to love Vietnamese food and to grow what he needs when he cannot find it fresh. Charlie showed him how to raise some of the staples of the old-fashioned Kentucky garden—Brandywine tomatoes, yellow crookneck squash, and turnip greens. And Jacinda's father, a preacher and gardener, introduced Thai to pole beans, broccoli, potatoes, and blackberries.

Borrowing from the traditions of their elders, Thai and Jacinda are building a life together. But they also glean new ideas from seed catalogs, public library books, and the Internet. They used Craigslist to find wood for a raised bed. Thai is hooked on a Japanese gardener's videos available on YouTube. And video streaming gave them access to the documentary film *Food, Inc.,* which has profoundly changed their gardening practices and their attitude toward the worldwide agribusiness food system. "After watching *Food, Inc.,* we learned about Monsanto.[87] We are transitioning to organic gardening this year," Thai said. "I believe it is healthier than putting chemicals onto your plants. We started composting. We use neem oil.

We are going to try using soy meal and bonemeal and make our own fertilizer." The documentary is also an effective exposé of the poultry industry's unsanitary and cruel processes. Thai and Jacinda now gather fresh eggs each day from five breeds of chickens—Wyandotte, Rhode Island Red, Partridge Rock, Astralorp, and Amber Link—that they raise in their backyard. In the spring of 2013, Thai became a beekeeper.

Thai's philosophy of gardening might be summed up by his own advice: "Keep on growing" and "Keep on learning." Charlie, though, remains Thai's muse. "He is a stair or stepping-stone for me," Thai explained. "He plants a garden every year. If he can do it, I can do it." Thai also credits Charlie with allowing him to experiment. But the desire to experiment originates in Thai's restless mind. No test, no trial and observation is beneath him, especially if it will inform his gardening practices. "You take your kitchen leftovers—scraps—throw it out in the ground, cover it up, the worms eat it. You produce less waste. Our garbage can, we take it out every two weeks. Our neighbor takes out two garbage cans every week." Thai said, "When I stop learning, I find that I get bored easily."

In Thai and Jacinda's garden is a persimmon tree. It is one of Thai's experiments. The persimmon, or *hong,* like the *nhan* of Thai's childhood, is a traditional Vietnamese fruit. Persimmons are presented as gifts to family members and are offered at ancestral altars. Thai described it as "an Asian variety" but said that "it is grafted on an American persimmon tree. That's why it is still alive." Someday, perhaps when he is silver-haired like Charlie, Thai will have a memory of the *nhan* and the persimmon-*hong* whispering to him that a garden—his garden—once grew both. And it will remind him that he is obliged to share what he can with someone walking by his garden.

Malabar spinach (also known as Indian spinach or Ceylon spinach), *Basella alba,* growing up the fence in Thai Tran's garden.

THE TOMATO REBELLION

Bill Stewart

I HAD NEVER MET most of the gardeners I interviewed for this book, but Bill Stewart and I go way back. He was part of the back-to-the-land movement of the 1960s and '70s, living in Estill County, where I moved, fresh with a library science degree, to run the public library in 1978. In those days the county was home to many young people who were trying to live sustainably off the land because they rejected the values embedded in America's consumer culture. They wanted to "drop out." A large contingent hailed from suburban Maryland, but the Lexington, Louisville, and Cincinnati areas were also represented. However, Bill was the only back-to-the-lander I knew who came from the land, temporarily left it, but then wanted to return.

Growing up on Stinking Creek in Knox County in the 1950s on his Stewart grandparents' farm, Bill Stewart is part of the last generation in eastern Kentucky in which farm life was often a common bond. He also came of age at the end of the 1960s and found himself a part of the sweeping social change in the United States. Environmentalism, feminism, the war in Vietnam, Lyndon Johnson's War on Poverty, the back-to-the-land movement, and youth's challenges to parental authority all affected Bill. The politics of his generation, combined with his early agricultural upbringing, created a complex person who still confidently walks a path of his own making. He does so with a keen sense of humor and an understanding of how seeming contradictions have informed his life and his gardens.

Bill's mother was a schoolteacher from Clay County, where she met Bill's father, who was working for a coal company, selling coal. Bill was born in 1949 and is the oldest of twenty grandchildren—"the oldest son of an oldest son of an oldest son." His grandparents' farm had been in the family since just after the Revolutionary War. The farm was large, containing rich bottomland and probably 120 cultivated acres. In eastern Kentucky, that is not a hardscrabble farm. At midcentury they were, on one hand, embracing the new agricultural tools such as hybridized seeds and chemical pesticides and, on the other hand, still growing field corn to grind into meal for the household cornbread. The families were straddling two worlds.

Even though his father was choosing the coal business over farming, Bill's parents built a house on the farm and began to raise their family. At first the families gardened together and Bill provided labor for his grandfather's farming operations. "The garden was probably one hundred feet by four hundred feet, with huge mounds of potatoes, corn, [and] probably eighty heads of cabbage, and the grandchildren's job as soon as they were big enough to hoe was to hoe. When I wasn't expected to be in the garden, my grandfather would grab us and make us bale hay or catch cows that had gotten out. [Another] job I had was to go out with a BB gun and assassinate the birds that were eating the cherries."

When Bill was about ten, his mother began to raise a garden separately from her in-laws. He said, "I think she wanted to grow what she wanted to grow in quantities that she wanted to grow, and eastern Kentucky is matriarchal in that sense. I suspect she wanted her own place so she could grow Big Boy [tomatoes] instead of Better Boys if she wanted to. It was just a smaller version of exactly the same garden. Potatoes, corn, beans, onions, cabbage—oh, I can see it—tomatoes. I remember the excitement she felt when she got one of the relatives to turn the soil over to start the garden. I suspect to her it was like a fresh palette to start painting on. I remember seeing my mother coming out of the garden soaking wet with sweat, and she was producing five times as many tomatoes as we could can, process, and consume. And she'd give them away. It was the act of growing the things—modern hybrid vegetables—and harvesting them that was rewarding for her."

But Bill's memories of his childhood garden experiences are mostly negative. He recalled, "One of my jobs was to pick the potato bugs off the potatoes and drop them in one of those brown Clorox jugs, and I just hated doing that. You're standing out there in the middle of the field, it's hot, you're sweating, you want to go swimming, and then you gotta hoe after that." Even though Bill disliked all the hard labor, particularly as a teenager, he never bucked his parents or grandparents. "An act of rebellion was sort of shooting yourself in the foot, because you ate those cows and you ate that corn. You ate those potatoes. It never would have occurred to me to have wasted something or let it go to pot." Bill did rebel. He just saved it for later.

The ethos of land as a resource to be exploited but also to be revered has a long history in the United States. Possibly nowhere is this paradox more highlighted than in the central Appalachian coalfields where Bill grew up. When Bill left his home in the mountains to attend Centre College in Danville, he was able to more freely wrestle with this contradiction. He had grown up in a family for whom self-reliance based on agrarian practices was held in high esteem and more or less still in place. But he could not ignore the growing destruction in his own backyard from coal mining. He reflected, "Driving back and seeing big gashes in the mountains and strip mines that had emptied out water into the creeks and killed all the fish, it seemed to me to be an environmental disaster in the making, and I was horrified. I was glad to get out of eastern Kentucky with people throwing their garbage in the creeks and anti-intellectual feelings. All that was so hard for me."

By that time, Bill's father had his own coal company. His method was strip-mining, and like many other small independent operators during this period, he was accumulating a sizable wealth. The 1973 OPEC oil embargo had caused the price of and demand for coal to rise significantly. Bill's connection to his homeplace and, especially to his father, became seriously strained. His political beliefs were crystallizing. As Bill put it, "I was going to stop strip-mining, eliminate poverty, and stop the Vietnam War in my spare time."

Eventually he moved to Carrollton, Georgia, where he entered graduate school at West Georgia College to study psychology. In looking for a place to live, Bill landed in a communal household with other students. "[They] had a huge vegetable garden with vegetables I didn't recognize, like peanuts and okra and Mississippi Silver Crowder peas. I literally went out and didn't know what ninety percent of their stuff in their garden was. You have to figure out how to cook those crowder peas and those peanuts, and I added my own tomatoes and corn. And there was a dairy across the street that you could get raw milk. There were fifteen mangy, scrawny chickens, and eventually somebody gave us a pig. We took the garbage from the school cafeteria and fed the pigs. We were living off the land. We were getting by. We were living as a community."

Bill's household tried to live entirely by a subsistence, do-it-yourself philosophy. The collective decided to butcher their hog. Bill was the only householder who had actually witnessed such an event. "I was so disinterested in how to kill a chicken and kill a pig when I was a kid that I tried to get away from doing it, and I certainly didn't closely observe the process. I knew that once you shot the pig you had to cut its throat and hang it up and bleed it and then you had to dip it in boiling water, but I didn't know that if you left it in boiling water longer than a couple of minutes that the hair would set up. So we had to shave the pig with an electric razor. We read *Foxfire,* but it didn't tell us how long we were supposed to leave the stupid pig in there. So you know it was an odd bastardization of your own childhood and reading *Foxfire* while the pig is laying there dead."

While Bill's ties to Kentucky were frayed at times, something kept drawing him back. He returned with a master's degree in clinical psychology and took a job in the state capital as an advocate for disabled people. But the pull of his back-to-the-land experience during graduate school was strong. He soon quit his job and moved to Estill County into what he described as "an old uninhabitable house with no windows." He lived on a hilltop farm with poor soil for ten years experimenting with a variety of vegetables and other adventures in a self-sustainable life. "We tried to grow bees, and they flew away. We tried to grow rabbits, and they hopped away. And the foxes ate our chickens." But it was there that he began a lifetime passion of raising heirloom vegetables and doing it organically. He read *Mother Earth News* and the *Last Whole Earth Catalog,* but it was his neighbor, Frank Stone, an old-timer and native of the county, who showed Bill the way. He said, "[Frank] had a kind of beans that were corn-field beans that you could plant in the corn; he called [them] tobacco worm beans because they were little short, fat beans. But they had been in his family for, I'm guessing, generations, and here were these beans that you just stuck them in the ground right next to the corn and you could grow two things at once and they were bred for that purpose. And they tasted good."

With his buddy Joe, a fellow back-to-the-lander, Bill tried some un-usual economic strategies. "I remember *Mother Earth News* said sell mistle-toe for a cash crop. So we harvested all this mistletoe by shooting it out of trees with a borrowed shotgun and went to Lexington and put our mistletoe out for everybody. We didn't sell a nickel's worth." They did not give up. "Another article said to cut up old rubber tires with a chain-saw and that makes good shingles, but they didn't mention not to get ra-dial tires with steel belts in them. We destroyed the chainsaw." Still another experiment involved putting into practice a common principle of the back-to-the-land movement: to stop consuming and start produc-ing. "[We] were going to get out of the industrial agricultural complex by not buying sugar. We tried to grow sugar beets so we wouldn't have to buy sugar. And the sugar beets, of course, took one look at where they were growing and committed suicide."

Bill now lives in Lexington, gardening organically in his backyard and in a large plot out in the Fayette County countryside. His experience in Estill County, though hard at times with no running water and a drafty, cold house, gave him a deep and varied knowledge about gardening. He is not afraid to try fennel, edamame, or artichokes along with his stable of heirloom vegetables. "What I took away was the understanding that I can grow almost anything that I want to. Except sugar beets."

Though Bill's history is probably not the one his parents envisioned, his life has circled back to his beginnings on his grandparent's farm, where his father still lives. Like his mother, he had to make his own gardens, and like she once did, he grows more than his family can use, giving the excess to his neighbors and friends. And it is the garden that feeds his son, Will, his wife, Mary, and now his father, too. "My father is ninety years old, and he steals my vegetables. I took him to a Bob Evans restaurant, and the hostess said, 'Mr. Stewart, those were such good turnips. I really appreciate that.' He stole my turnips," Bill said, relishing the lighthearted story of his father posing as the gardener who had grown the turnips. But these

vegetable exchanges also signaled a deeper change in a once contentious father-son relationship. "I gave him some tomatoes the other day," Bill said. "You can imagine what they look like—little black tomatoes and streak tomatoes and lumpy yellow tomatoes, cat-faced tomatoes. He went, 'Ugh. Don't you have any just regular red tomatoes?' But he came back a few days later and said, 'You know those little black ones that are kind of round and real dark, do you have any more of those?'" Bill smiled, indicating a victory a long time in coming. "He's wanting the heirloom tomatoes."[88]

Bill was unable to stop strip-mining or eradicate poverty, but he is still a rebel healing the land and feeding people—one delicious, organic vegetable at a time. Who knows what can happen when your own father shifts his loyalties from a hybridized Big Boy to an old-time Black Russian tomato. There could be a revolution.

EPILOGUE

Belonging

ALONG ABOUT THE TIME I was beginning to interview Kentucky gardeners for what was to become *Row by Row,* I copied down a sentence from Jeff Goodell's *Big Coal: The Dirty Secret behind America's Energy Future.*[89] It reads, "One of the triumphs of modern life is our ability to distance ourselves from the simple facts of our own existence." He was referring to energy sources and the way in which we turn on a light switch without thinking about the origins of that light. This "triumph of modern life" allows us to deny the hidden costs of our reliance on fossil fuels—the cost to the environment, to the people and communities where the extractive process takes place, and to the general public's health, safety, and security. It is no stretch to replace the phrase Big Coal with Big Food or Big Agriculture, because too many of us have forgotten or know little about where food comes from. And Big Food has hidden costs not unlike those of Big Coal. But home vegetable gardeners have not surrendered this knowledge or memory. Gardeners are steeped in the "simple facts of our own existence," from Jennifer Eskew (who as a young adult set out a few five-gallon buckets in which to grow tomatoes in downtown Lexington) to Betty Decker (who in her sixties still plants a massive garden in her native Wayne County).

The hidden costs of our industrialized food system have been well documented by films such as *Food, Inc.* (2009), *Super Size Me* (2004), and

The Corporation (2005), as well as books including Barbara Kingsolver's *Animal, Vegetable, Miracle: A Year of Food Life,* Michael Pollan's *Omnivore's Dilemma: A Natural History of Four Meals,* and Eric Schlosser's *Fast Food Nation: The Dark Side of the All-American Meal.* Many of the gardeners in *Row by Row* speak eloquently about the injuries to the land, water, and people caused by Big Food. But more often they talk about what they are doing in their gardens to undermine and reverse this course. They discuss organic gardening practices, the superior taste of fresh vegetables, the health advantages of homegrown food, and how gardens improve local food security and household economies. They point out that gardening provides community and familial continuity and also fosters feelings of independence and pride. More than a few voice their spiritual connection to working the land and growing their food. And still others extend their own growing know-how as a way to help others. Instead of home vegetable gardening having costs, it has benefits.

One of these benefits, I believe, is a sense of belonging. Through the gardeners I have come to see that belonging to a place, to a community, to the land, to a family, to a history, or to a movement, is one of the beneficial, though sometimes opaque, effects of home vegetable gardening. If growing our own food keeps us more closely connected to the "simple facts of our own existence," maybe it is belonging that elevates existence to a life more fully lived—in and outside of our gardens.

Belonging is a tricky thing. It can oppress or liberate us—sometimes both. Belonging to a group can make some of us feel safe and wanted, while at the same time excluding those who do not fit or adhere to the group's parameters. Belonging can create both harmony and violence. The desire to belong can make us grasping or giving. Belonging often feels as if it will last forever, but there is always the possibility of a terrible interruption—death, job loss, catastrophic weather, war, sickness, environmental disaster, someone goes off the deep end. Sometimes these kinds of disturbances render belonging more urgent and even generate new forms of belonging.

Gardeners are not immune from the paradoxes of belonging or the hardship that life brings. The lives portrayed in *Row by Row* are proof. These Kentuckians have sustained family loss and breakups, disability, poverty, racism, displacement, cultural dissonance, failed experiments, political conflict, unfair traditions, and broken traditions. But making a garden for the first time or the fiftieth, as their stories show, can provide a way to circle around, to hold on, to chart a new course, to soothe a weary spirit, to learn something new, to experience unadulterated joy. That is the work that both gardening and belonging can do for us. The garden feeds us with more than food.

For Gladys and Walsa Blanton, gardening is one of the most powerful ties they maintain with their three deceased children. It is no exaggeration to say that their garden is where these children belong. Saunda Coleman, who was orphaned at a young age, sees the plants in her garden "like a little family" to which she belongs. Jennifer Eskew finds belonging in her garden memories and in reenacting her family's food practices. Working together in a Cooperative Extension community garden, Marisol Ortiz helps her fellow Latino gardeners develop roots in Kentucky. Gloria and Don Williams, who do not wonder whether they belong in the place where they and their parents have always lived, use this security to forge alternative gardening and social practices. As Gloria said, "Everything doesn't have to be McDonald's."

Linda Rose, Dave Kennedy, and Janice Musick belong to an ethos of caring for the environment and step gently to keep their footprints light. Sharing with neighbors the fruits of her garden is a belonging place for Mae Raney Sons. Joe Trigg believes that doing good things is the purpose of belonging; this belief spurs him to engage young people's interest in gardening and farming. In Bev May's mind, belonging is something you earn through reciprocity with your neighbors and your land. As a little boy trying to learn English in his new home, Thai Tran found it by watching a gardener work each day as he passed to and from elementary school. Jashu and Kasan Patel locate belonging by growing the foods that they want to eat, connecting them back to their agricultural past in India. Mattie and Bill Mack belong in Meade County because there is nowhere else they want to be than on the farm they worked hard to get and keep. Though Gary Millwood passed in 2013, he will belong to every garden where an old-time tomato seed that he helped save is planted. Bill Stewart and Tom Collins belong to the old practice of rearranging tradition. Rossneau Ealom will always belong to his beloved Loretta because they made gardens together.

Perhaps it was one of the first gardeners I interviewed for this project who sowed the seed that has grown into these last words in *Row by Row*. Bruce Mundy was born in 1953 into a large African American family who raised vegetables in their Lexington yards.[90] Bruce has spent much of his adult life working with children and teens on organic vegetable gardens and other ecological projects. Known as Brother Bruce in many circles, he is a philosophical thinker who engages a variety of intellectual and spiritual traditions. "I'm not trying to save the earth," he told me. "I'm trying to save

myself. The earth would be much better off without us. It would not pollute the water, it would not pollute the air. But we do. And because we have disconnected ourselves from everything that we do, we will pollute water and drink it, pollute the air, then breathe it. There is some insanity there."

Bruce continued by offering an alternative view. "All things are connected. [Indigenous people] said that God was in the water, was in the air, was in the rock, was in the tree, that God was in all things. Gardening makes connections. While I like gardening for its food value, I would be lying [if I said] that's the only reason I do it. I want people to eat good, don't get me wrong. But I know its restorative value. In the garden there's restoration for a sometimes troubled spirit."

When my spirit is troubled, I try to remember the sheer joy on Betty Decker's face as she explained to me the meaning she derives from her gigantic vegetable garden. "Doesn't it give you a really good feeling, too," she asked, "when you can stand back and look at all these beautiful plants and say, 'This is mine and I grew it with my own hands'?"

Many people would look at Betty Decker and Bruce Mundy and see very different lives. That is true. But what is also true is that their lives meet in the garden. They do not see any "hidden costs" to gardening, only benefits. If they were composing a "Gardener's Creed" together, I think it would sound like this: Grow food with our own hands, connect to the elements that sustain us, restore our collective spirit, and belong to each other.

NOTES

1. A fodder shock is constructed from the dried-out plant after the ears of corn have been removed. The cornstalks are pulled from the ground and stood upright, crisscrossed at the top, and around an imaginary circle. This process is repeated until a rather large thick tepee shape is formed. The shocks can be used to feed livestock in the winter. Today many people recognize a fodder shock as an iconic fall and Halloween decoration.

2. To "sucker" tobacco means to remove the side shoots. Suckering and topping (i.e., removing) the flowering head causes the plant's energy to go into developing bigger leaves on one main stalk.

3. "County Summary Highlights," in *Census of Agriculture* (Washington, DC: U.S. Department of Agriculture, National Agricultural Statistics Service, 1992, 1997, 2002).

4. Bodwank is approximately 150 miles (240 kilometers) north of Bombay (Mumbai). Kasan told me that a small farm in Gujarat at that time might have been only an acre-sized plot, far smaller than what would be considered a small farm in Kentucky.

5. Vijay Prashad, *The Karma of Brown Folk* (Minneapolis: University of Minnesota Press, 2000), 78. Prashad's work (especially chapter 3, "Of the Origins of Desis," pp. 69–83) informed my thinking about the immigration process for South Asians and how a host of social and economic forces in India, the United States, and even Great Britain influenced the possibility and timing of Jashu and Kasan's immigration.

6. The closest store that sells specialized ingredients for Indian cuisines, including produce, is in Lexington, about thirty minutes away.

7. I learned, just as this book was going to press, that Forest had died at home on October 11, 2013.

8. Today, most tobacco farmers no longer start their own plants; they buy them from a supplier who grows the tobacco sets but does not necessarily raise tobacco as a crop. These sets (or plants) are most often grown in greenhouses in hydroponic "float beds." The tobacco beds that were second nature to Forest are now a thing of the past.

9. Mae's mother was unusual in growing wheat. The U.S. Agricultural Census for Menifee County documents only three farms reporting winter wheat threshed in 1929, twelve in 1934, four in 1939, and only two by 1945.

10. Nuts that fall from trees onto the forest floor and provide food for animals are known as "mast."

11. Because I was unaware of and could not readily confirm the existence of a beech tree blight in Kentucky, I contacted Thomas Barnes, an extension professor, at the University of Kentucky's Department of Forestry. In an e-mail exchange on May 13, 2013, he wrote that there is a "beech bark disease which is caused by a fungus." It has been present in the United States since the late 1890s but has not spread to Kentucky, to his knowledge. Dr. Barnes also explained that beech trees do not "produce good [nut] crops until they are about 50 years old" and that even healthy beech trees in the forest do not consistently produce a viable crop of nuts annually. Those characteristics of the beech in combination with the "wholesale clear-cut[ting]" of eastern Kentucky forests, "beginning in the 1920s, leaving no standing timber," seems a more likely cause, he thought, of the beech nuts' demise that Mae Sons remembered.

12. A teepee-shaped construction made of the dried stalks of corn after the ears have been harvested. See also note 1.

13. The wooden barrels looked similar to the ones in which bourbon is aged—white oak staves with metal bands encircling the circumference. The barrels that Mae's family used were recycled: originally they were the shipping containers for glass jugs of vinegar. The Raneys also used these barrels to pickle corn and cucumbers and to make sauerkraut (from cabbage).

14. Stark's is a reputable and long-standing mail order source for fruit trees and berries still in business today.

15. Dried apples were prized by mountain cooks and eaters because they were used in the filling for fried pies and for the special "apple stack cake."

16. "Natural food advocates maintain that sulfured fruit is harmful and that sulfuring is done mainly for cosmetic reasons. There is currently no evidence to substantiate this claim. Research shows that sulfuring retards spoilage and darkening of fruits, lessens the contamination by insects during sun drying, and reduces the loss of vitamins A and C." Deanna DeLong, *How to Dry Foods,* rev. ed. (New York: Home Books, 2006), 25.

17. A slip is a plant that is started from the leafy vine that sprouts, particularly at the end of the winter, from the "eyes" on the sweet potato.

18. After tobacco is cut at its stalk in the field, several stalks are brought together and speared with a tobacco stick, which is then hung in a barn with good ventilation, until it is ready, about four to eight weeks later, to be stripped. This is called "curing" the tobacco.

19. Planting "by the signs" of the zodiac or "by the moon" is an ancient practice in which gardeners who follow the "cycles" believe that the vitality and productivity of their vegetable crops are determined, in part, by the moon's revolution around the earth each month. Planting, weeding, and even pruning are determined by the phases of the moon. There is not yet scientific validation for this practice, but many gardeners and farmers continue to plant according to the system's tenets. For an edifying discussion on

the relationship between science, empiricism, and "moon planting" see *Rodale's Ultimate Encyclopedia of Organic Gardening* (Emmaus, PA: Rodale Books, 2009), 40–41.

20. Ciro and Maria Prudente's first language is Spanish. Ciro, especially, also speaks English, and he spoke both languages during the interview, while Maria spoke primarily Spanish. I do not speak Spanish. Margie Hernandez, who is on the staff of the Russell County Cooperative Extension, generously interpreted throughout this interview, conducted in December 2009. She also exchanged e-mails with me in May 2013 to clarify a few details I had missed during the interview.

21. The website for the U.S. Department of Agriculture describes its Cooperative Extension System "as a nationwide, non-credit educational network. Each U.S. state and territory has a state office at its land-grant university and a network of local or regional offices. These offices are staffed by one or more experts who provide useful, practical, and research-based information to agricultural producers, small business owners, youth, consumers, and others in rural areas and communities of all sizes."

22. A profile of Marisol Ortiz appears elsewhere in this volume.

23. When I returned the following June with a photographer, I got to meet the new baby, Jennifer Ruby Prudente, who was sleeping in the shade while Ciro and Maria picked vegetables from their garden.

24. Rossneau told me that the church remains active today but most of the African American families have sold their land and moved away to Hopkinsville and Louisville and to other states such as Tennessee, Ohio, Indiana, and Virginia.

25. Kentucky State University (KSU) is a historically black university and is also a land-grant university. KSU has a vital Small Farms program with an arm that focuses particularly on "resource-limited," minority, and women farmers. Rossneau attends KSU's annual conference focused on these small farmers.

26. In November 2011, Jennifer moved to Nashville, where she started a job as a technical writer and editor and a new garden with raised beds.

27. A community garden usually consists of parcels of land assigned to various individual gardeners. These plots are part of a larger tract of publicly or privately owned land. Sometimes a nominal fee for use is charged, and often the garden is governed by a set of rules about use of pesticides and fertilizers, watering, weeding, and harvesting. In some cases one large garden, rather than parcels, is worked together by a collective of gardeners.

28. A food desert is a geographic area in which the residents have little or no access to stores that sell fresh, healthy food. Food deserts go hand in hand with large concentrations of low-income and poor people; although the term is mostly used to describe urban areas, in my mind, Kentucky has its share of food deserts in its small towns and rural areas. A community garden in the middle of a food desert can make a difference, particularly when food preservation techniques, such as canning, are incorporated into the project.

29. Margie Hernandez is on staff at the Russell County Cooperative Extension. She grew up in McCreary County. She married a Cuban who was raised in Puerto Rico, and for sixteen years they lived in his hometown, where Margie learned to speak Spanish. She and her husband now live in rural Casey County. Besides participating as both an interpreter and a gardener in the project, she was also an interpreter for interviews I conducted with two Spanish-speaking gardeners.

30. Head Start is a federal government program for low-income preschool children to prepare them as students—intellectually, emotionally, physically, and socially. It was part of President Lyndon Johnson's 1964 War on Poverty legislation.

31. Marisol moved to Bowling Green, Kentucky, late in 2012 because Fruit of the Loom once again transferred her husband. She has continued her work with migrant families and Head Start there.

32. According to an article by M. Michael Miller in *Minerals Yearbook* (Reston, VA: U.S. Geological Survey, 2012), "fluorspar is used directly or indirectly to manufacture such products as aluminum, gasoline, insulating foams, plastics, refrigerants, steel, and uranium fuel." The United States had no active fluorspar mines in 2012; imports supplied U.S. industry's need.

33. The miners in this family have worked in underground coal mines in Webster and Hopkins Counties, approximately twenty-five miles from their home.

34. At the time of our interview in May 2009, Donna and Larry were the only certified Master Gardeners in Crittenden County. To receive the designation of "Master Gardener," one must attend a series of classes, usually taught by the local extension agent, pass an examination, and perform at least thirty hours of community service related to gardening. To maintain this certification, one must complete fifteen hours of community service annually.

35. A good source about attracting birds to the garden is *Gardening for the Birds* by Thomas G. Barnes (Lexington: University Press of Kentucky, 1999).

36. She is referring to racial segregation of the time, one so complete that African Americans could not use the same entrance as white patients when procuring the services of a white doctor.

37. The Tuskegee Institute in Alabama, founded in 1881 and run by Booker T. Washington until he died in 1915, was primarily focused on training teachers and preparing African Americans to work in the skilled trades and in agricultural science. By the late 1950s, when Miss Mattie was a student there, the curriculum included a college degree-granting program and professional schools such as veterinary medicine.

38. The Lincoln Institute was a boarding school for black high school students operating from 1912 to the 1960s. It was created by Berea College as a response to the 1904 passage of the Day Law in Kentucky, outlawing racially integrated educational institutions. Berea College in Madison County, Kentucky, had been committed to interracial education since the end of the Civil War.

39. The farm at thirty-five thousand dollars was what Miss Mattie called a "walkout" sale. The Bell family left everything, including farm implements, animals, and even some antique furniture.

40. If it was hard for the Macks to find land that they would be allowed to buy, the fact that they still own it, free and clear, is another feat they have managed. See the three-part series "Torn from the Land" by Todd Lewan and Dolores Barclay, published by the Associated Press on December 2, 3, and 9, 2001, which documents "a pattern in which black Americans were cheated out of their land or driven from it through intimidation, violence and even murder" for "150-plus years."

41. Cushaw is a type of winter squash.

42. A green bean plant that grows in the bunch style. Bunch, or bush, beans grow up to two feet tall, do not require staking, and are usually planted in rows.

43. Besides Joe, his brother Erron and his cousin Rodney live in Glasgow. Brothers Cedric and Christopher are spread out from California to Louisville, Kentucky. The land they cultivate includes an eighty-six-acre farm in Barren County, bought by Trigg Enterprise. There they raise beef cattle but no tobacco. Inside the city limits of Glasgow, Trigg Enterprise owns twelve more acres to grow field vegetables, such as corn. The Trigg homeplace, where the greenhouse is located, consists of two acres. Their entire holdings total one hundred acres.

44. I interviewed Joe Trigg in the fall of 2009 after his first season of F2CC. He supplied the more recent history of F2CC in an e-mail to me dated April 17, 2013.

45. "Fertigation" is water plus fertilizer.

46. Joe is now using five-gallon white plastic buckets (similar to those containing drywall mud) instead of bags.

47. This method requires that certain plants, "companion" plants, be located in close proximity to one another in the field or the garden. Companion planting has especially been used to either deter or trap pests or attract beneficial insects. Joe told me that he plants basil, for example, among his tomatoes to good effect.

48. In particular, Joe releases insects—such as ladybugs and praying mantises—into his greenhouses and fields as natural predators to less desirable insects that damage crops. Joe pointed out that this is a "balancing act," since "bad" bugs need to be present for the "good" bugs to have something to eat.

49. For a discussion of planting by the signs, see note 19.

50. Gary died at the end of May 2013, just before the gardening season went into full swing.

51. In more recent years, the homes that remain have changed focus. Gary said they are "treatment oriented" and provide services for children with drug and behavioral problems.

52. The Bellewood farm is located at Anchorage, to the east of downtown Louisville. Today it is part of the greater Louisville area. "The Bellewood Presbyterian Home for

Children began in 1853 as the Louisville Orphans' Home Society with a facility on what is now called Kentucky Street. When the Presbyterians divided after the Civil War, the property also was split. The Southern Presbyterians soon moved their orphanage to Anchorage, where they shared land with the Bellewood Seminary, a school for girls. Early in its existence, the orphanage began to accept needy children who were not themselves Presbyterians." Louis B. Weeks, *Kentucky Presbyterians* (Atlanta: John Knox Press, 1983), 152. In a volume produced to celebrate the sesquicentennial of Kentucky Presbyterianism (1802–1952), the children who live at Bellewood are described as being "on an equal footing with all others"; they "attend . . . the public school, one block away at Anchorage, one of the best in Jefferson County, and are regular at Bible School and Worship at the Presbyterian Church, next door." *Source Book of Historical Material for Ministers, Editors, Speakers, and Study Groups*, 45.

53. The Southern Exposure Seed Exchange website (www.southernexposure.com) describes the Aunt Lou tomato this way: "82 days. (Indeterminate) [Heirloom carried through the Underground Railroad by an unnamed black man as he crossed to freedom in Ripley, OH, from KY. Seeds were passed on to Aunt Lou, who passed them on to her great nephew, and eventually on to heirloom tomato enthusiast Gary Millwood.] Dark pink, tangy and juicy, 4–12 oz. fruits. Sparse foliage." I interviewed Gary near the end of August, and naturally he had prepared a lunch for me from his late summer harvest of tomatoes and peppers. "Food with family and friends is my gift," Gary told me. The Aunt Lou was special.

54. Shucky beans are dried green beans. Fresh beans are usually strung together with thread and hung up for the drying process. An apple stack cake is a revered delicacy in eastern Kentucky. It is made of many thin layers of spice cake with apple filling between each layer. Arguably, reconstituted dried apples make the best and most authentic filling.

55. A nonprofit organization, PRIDE also works on water quality issues by installing septic tanks and eliminating straight-line pipes, which often drain home sewage directly into waterways. It was the brainchild of Kentucky congressional representative Hal Rogers and receives funding from local government and from federal sources such as the Appalachian Regional Commission.

56. "Brought-on" is like "store-bought"; put another way, the terms refer to something decidedly not local.

57. The demonstrations at the Chicago Democratic Convention in 1968, coupled with the escalation of the Vietnam War, ultimately caused the New Left and its representative body, Students for a Democratic Society (SDS), to fracture into more ideologically driven groups, particularly influenced by Maoism. These "hard politics" to which Dave refers signaled the diminishing influence of the communal, nonconformist ethos of the hippies and the rise of more sectarian leftist politics, symbolized by such groups as the Weather Underground.

58. The Farm, located near Summertown, Tennessee, and founded by hippies from San Francisco in 1971, is still in existence today.

59. The English have worked on leafy greens concentrate since World War II, when preventing malnourishment was paramount because food supplies were interrupted by blockades.

60. Find Your Feet is still a functioning organization, though, according to Kennedy, its focus has shifted from leaf concentrate to financial and logistical support for rural development projects in India and southern Africa, including Malawi.

61. In 2011 Leaf for Life published his *Twenty-First Century Greens: Leaf Vegetables in Nutrition and Sustainable Agriculture,* a "resource book."

62. Bombay was renamed Mumbai in 1996, but both Seema and Ashish refer to it as the former. I use "Bombay" in this essay. Today it is the most populous city in India and the fourth most populous city in the world.

63. Allahabad is in the northern Indian state of Uttar Pradesh.

64. Seema explained to me in an e-mail follow-up to our interview that in order to practice medicine in the United States, doctors from other countries must repeat medical school final exams and complete a one-year internship followed by a three-year residency.

65. Ichiban is a Japanese eggplant that is long and slender.

66. Native plants are those that are indigenous to an area or have naturalized over a long period of time. In general, but not always, they require less care and intervention by the gardener than do plants that are not native. Exotic plants are the opposite. They are plants that do not naturally exist in an area. In Seema's case, her exotic plants tend to be tropical or subtropical, which is why she must keep them in pots and, during Kentucky's cool and freezing months, move them inside for protection.

67. Martha and Adan's first language is Spanish. Adan speaks English but preferred to mainly speak Spanish during the interview. Martha spoke primarily Spanish. I do not speak Spanish. Margie Hernandez, who is on the staff of the Russell County Cooperative Extension, generously interpreted throughout this interview, conducted in December 2009. She also exchanged e-mails with me in May 2013 to verify spelling of proper names.

68. See the profile of Marisol Ortiz elsewhere in this volume.

69. She is referring to staff in the Russell County Cooperative Extension office: Pam York, county extension agent for family and consumer sciences; Julie Beckman, program assistant; and Wanda Miick, small farm program assistant. As of 2013 Pam York and Wanda Miick still worked at the Extension office, though Wanda had recently changed to part time.

70. Paul clarified: "At one time [the farm was said to be] five hundred acres. I can only account for about three hundred acres. A lot of it was sold off." Today Paul and Valeria own 135 acres of the original farm, and other family members have retained about a hundred acres.

71. Kentucky death records show that Edward Mills died on November 18, 1934, at the estimated age of seventy-three (Death Certificate file no. 28344). Census records indicate that Edward's occupation was "farmer" and that he could read and write.

72. Mr. Cummins farmed well into his eighties. He died in 2002 at age eighty-nine.

73. Bt, or *Bacillus thuringiensis,* is a biological pesticide that is often used by organic gardeners and farmers on the worms that attack broccoli, cabbage, and other cruciferous vegetables; it is considered safe for pollinators, animals, and people. Neem is a botanical pesticide and fungicide extracted from the seeds of the neem tree, a native to India.

74. Paul is referring to the summer of 2009.

75. After a field or garden has been turned (i.e., plowed), a harrow is used to break up the large ridges of dirt produced by the plow. A disc harrow is an implement attached to the rear of a tractor, made of metal discs with sharp edges and mounted on a long rod. When the harrow is engaged, the discs turn, cutting up the plowed mounds into small clods in which seeds will be able to germinate and establish a strong root system.

76. Many Kentuckians, especially eastern Kentuckians, have long been dedicated bean savers. Families and communities often have a bean that is "their bean." Betty said that her great-grandmother grew the Granny Bell bean and asserted that "they taste like no other bean." The term *stick bean* means it is a pole bean that requires some kind of stake to wind around and grow upward. Betty and two of her three children who garden continue to grow and save the Granny Bell bean.

77. *Calabaza,* a Spanish word, is a broad term used for all squash and gourds. The calabaza I am referring to is a green pumpkin-like squash that keeps well.

78. In the upland area of Jessamine County where the Mezas live, the ridgetops are often flat, and "elevations of 950 to 1000 feet are common," according to a Kentucky Geological Survey website focused on the groundwater resources of Kentucky counties.

79. More recently, Jose is also working with the Thoroughbred horses his employer raises.

80. Remarkably, all but one of Jose's thirteen siblings live in Kentucky. And both his parents also live in Jessamine County.

81. Today the organization is known as Kentuckians for the Commonwealth. The broad form deed was a contract used by land speculators and coal companies in the late 1800s and into the early 1900s giving ownership of the mineral rights to the buyer while the seller retained only the surface rights. The owner of a broad form deed did not require permission from the surface owner to access below the surface and could retrieve the minerals by any means necessary, thereby rendering the surface unusable and even uninhabitable.

82. Sevin is not organic; it has commonly been used by home gardeners since the 1960s.

83. DDT was a widely used agricultural insecticide beginning after World War II until its use was banned in the United States in 1972. Rachel Carson's *Silent Spring,* published in 1962, is often credited with alerting the public to the dangers of such chemical pesticides.

84. The back-to-the-land movement in the United States in the 1960s and 1970s was built by those who rejected the requirements of a 9–5 job, who wanted to be more self-sufficient and live on a smaller scale, and who saw land and its cultivation—if done properly—as a means to change.

85. One of Thai's brothers died during the American-Vietnam War.

86. She and her family immigrated to Louisville, via California, in 2010.

87. In addition to genetically engineering and modifying seeds, Monsanto produces herbicides used globally in agribusiness. The United States used Agent Orange, made by Monsanto, as a defoliant in Vietnam during the war.

88. Bill's father, William S. Stewart, died at home on the family farm on November 24, 2010.

89. Jeff Goodell, *Big Coal: The Dirty Secret behind America's Energy Future* (New York: Houghton Mifflin Harcourt, 2006), xi.

90. A profile of Bruce Mundy is not included in this volume. However, our taped interview, conducted on March 16, 2009, is available and housed in the Louie B. Nunn Center for Oral History, Special Collections and Archives, University of Kentucky Libraries.